Property of
Haddon Heights
Public Library

AF802714

CEMENTVILLE

by Jane Martin

SAMUEL FRENCH, INC.
45 West 25th Street NEW YORK 10010
7623 Sunset Boulevard HOLLYWOOD 90046
LONDON *TORONTO*

HADDON HEIGHTS PUBLIC LIBRARY
608 STATION AVENUE
P. O. BOX 240
HADDON HEIGHTS, NEW JERSEY 08035-0240

Copyright © 1991 by Jane Martin

ALL RIGHTS RESERVED

CAUTION: Professionals and amateurs are hereby warned that CEMENTVILLE is subject to a royalty. It is fully protected under the copyright laws of the United States of America, the British Commonwealth, including Canada, and all other countries of the Copyright Union. All rights, including professional, amateur, motion pictures, recitation, lecturing, public reading, radio broadcasting, television, and the rights of translation into foreign languages are strictly reserved. In its present form the play is dedicated to the reading public only.

The amateur live stage performance rights to CEMENTVILLE are controlled exclusively by Samuel French, Inc., and royalty arrangements and licenses must be secured well in advance of presentation. PLEASE NOTE that amateur royalty fees are set upon application in accordance with your producing circumstances. When applying for a royalty quotation and license please give us the number of performances intended, dates of production, your seating capacity and admission fee. Royalties are payable one week before the opening performance of the play to Samuel French, Inc., at 45 W. 25th Street, New York, NY 10010; or at 7623 Sunset Blvd., Hollywood, CA 90046, or to Samuel French (Canada), Ltd., 80 Richmond Street East, Toronto, Ontario, Canada M5C 1P1.

Royalty of the required amount must be paid whether the play is presented for charity or gain and whether or not admission is charged.

Stock royalty quoted on application to Samuel French, Inc.

For all other rights than those stipulated above, apply to Alexander Speer, c/o Actors Theatre of Louisville, 316 W. Main St., Louisville, KY 40202.

Particular emphasis is laid on the question of amateur or professional readings, permission and terms for which must be secured in writing from Samuel French, Inc.

Copying from this book in whole or in part is strictly forbidden by law, and the right of performance is not transferable.

Whenever the play is produced the following notice must appear on all programs, printing and advertising for the play: "Produced by special arrangement with Samuel French, Inc."

Due authorship credit must be given on all programs, printing and advertising for the play.

ISBN 0 573 69247 5 Printed in the U.S.A.

No one shall commit or authorize any act or omission by which the copyright of, or the right to copyright, this play may be impaired.

No one shall make any changes in this play for the purpose of production.

Publication of this play does not imply availability for performance. Both amateurs and professionals considering a production are *strongly* advised in their own interests to apply to Samuel French, Inc., for written permission before starting rehearsals, advertising, or booking a theatre.

No part of this book may be reproduced, stored in a retrieval system, or transmitted in any form, by any means, now known or yet to be invented, including mechanical, electronic, photocopying, recording, videotaping, or otherwise, without the prior written permission of the publisher.

IMPORTANT BILLING AND CREDIT REQUIREMENTS

All producers of CEMENTVILLE *must* give credit to the Author of the Play in all programs distributed in connection with performances of the Play and in all instances in which the title of the Play appears for purposes of advertising, publicizing or otherwise exploiting the Play and/or a production. The name of the Author *must* also appear on a separate line, on which no other name appears, immediately following the title, and *must* appear in size of type not less than fifty percent the size of the title type.

All producers must also show the following credit in all programs distributed in connection with performances of the Play:

> "World premiere at the Actors Theatre of Louisville as part of the 1991 Humana Festival of New American Plays."

72930

Cementville produced by the Actors Theatre of Louisville, premiered at the 15th Annual Humana Festival of New American Plays, March 1991. It was directed by Jon Jory. The cast (in order of appearance) was:

DWAYNE PARDEE .... Jim Petersmith
TIGER .... Suzanna Hay
NOLA .... Corliss Preston
DANI .... Annette Helde
NETTY .... Adale O'Brien
LESSA .... Kimberley LaMarque
BIGMAN .... Fred Major
MOTHER CROCKER .... Sally Parrish
DOTTIE .... Peggity Price
DOLLY .... Cynthia Carle
MISS HARMON .... Jessica Jory
ONE-EYE DENEAUVE .... Bob Burrus
KID .... Lex Monson
EDDIE .... Tom Stechschulte

CHARACTERS

DWAYNE PARDEE, a wolf in wimp's clothing, 45
TIGER, at the end of a long rope, 35
NOLA, all the shrewd innocence of youth, 22
DANI, a tough talking frog in a small pond, 35
NETTY, mothers everything that moves, 40
BIGMAN, promoter, wrestler, hustler, fool, 40
LESSA, athlete in a cul-de-sac, 32
MOTHER, don't tread on me, 50
DOTTIE, wild beauty and bad karma, 28
DOLLY, sex and madness reconciled, 26
ONE-EYE DENEAUVE, country nightmares, 45
MISS HARMON, a little terrified order in chaos, 17
EDDIE, the Frankenstein monster, 42
KID, a boxer with a world view, 70

The play takes place in the locker room of a boxing arena in Cementville, Tennessee.

The time is the present.

ACT I

An empty, run-down locker room in an unused boxing arena in a small industrial city in Tennessee. Peeling plaster, water stains. Portions of the ceiling bubble ominously. One door with a twist lock leads in from an outside hallway. One door leads into a shower room the delicate would avoid. One door stands open revealing a broom closet partially filled with rotten, rolled up Venetian blinds and a decaying mop and bucket. Along the walls of the room stand lockers of two distinct periods. A ceiling fixture with three naked bulbs provides most of the illumination. Above the lockers there are posters ranging back to the 1950's naming fighters an aficionado might recognize. Some, mold has obliterated, some have inexplicably survived. The floor is littered with beer cans, Coke cups, newspapers and nasty drek. Several lockers stand open, revealing their own distressing mess. A small MAN in his forties walks past the door. A moment. HE returns and stands framed in the doorway looking in.

DWAYNE. Geez. (*Enters and stares around him.*) Geez, I don't know ...

(*A woman's VOICE is heard in the outside hall.*)

TIGER'S VOICE. Anybody home?

(DWAYNE starts out the door, realizes he is trapped, moves into the broom closet and closes himself in. TIGER appears in the doorway. SHE wears a tank top and jeans with an Elvis Presley jacket that reads "Taking Care of Business" on the back. SHE carries a flight bag, a cat-carrying case and a beer. SHE has a rolled up comic in her back pocket. She is around thirty-five. SHE surveys the room.)

TIGER. Son-of-a-bitch! (*SHE kicks a can.*) Hey, kid! (*Turns on LIGHT.*) Jeee-sus.

(A young GIRL enters. SHE wears shorts and a heavy metal T-shirt. SHE carries a push broom. She is seventeen or eighteen.)

NOLA. Yo.
TIGER. We supposed to dress in here?
NOLA. He said.
TIGER. We supposed to do it standin' up? (*Walking into the shower room.*)
NOLA. Huh?
TIGER. Benches.
NOLA. Right.
TIGER. You got benches?
NOLA. To sit down.
TIGER. Yeah.
NOLA. I don't know.
TIGER. (*Half pleased.*) There's a dead rat in the shower room.
NOLA. Showers don't work anyway.

TIGER. You seen a big man in a suit?

NOLA. On the pay phone two hours.

TIGER. Damn.

NOLA. Real agitated.

TIGER. Every time there's a man on a phone my life gets screwed up. You know was it a parole officer?

NOLA. No ma'am. (*Indicating the cat case.*) What's that?

TIGER. Family.

NOLA. (*Bending to look in.*) Kitty, kitty.

TIGER. It's a chihuahua. French kisses better than a man. You got a cigarette?

NOLA. Sure. (*Offers one.*)

TIGER. They use this crap hole for anything?

NOLA. Not since Jesus was a pup.

TIGER. Yeah? Look, go find the big man and tell him I don't dress standin' up. And get me a beer. Make that a six-pack.

NOLA. You the one on the poster?

TIGER. No, I ain't on the poster.

(Another WOMAN enters. She is in her late twenties and prettier in a worn way. SHE wears a sweater and a beret. SHE carries a container of fast food, a Pepsi, french fries and a half-eaten burrito.)

TIGER. She's on the poster.

DANI. (*Looking at the room.*) Are you kiddin' me?

TIGER. What's your name, kid?

NOLA. Nola.

TIGER. Nola, Tarzana Queen of the Jungle. Tarzana, Nola.

NOLA. Hey.

DANI. I'm not doing this.

TIGER. (*Experimentally opening lockers.*) Yeah?

DANI. I got a cleanliness clause.

TIGER. Rubbers. There's used rubbers in this locker.

DANI. Great.

TIGER. Well, I'm glad somebody was havin' fun.

NOLA. I was gonna, you know, sweep up, you know, but, whoa, he's got me hoppin'. (*No one speaks, SHE starts to leave.*) Six-pack.

DANI. Nola.

NOLA. Yo.

DANI. I'm Dani. You want my autograph?

NOLA. Yeah.

DANI. Clean this up.

NOLA. Yes ma'am. Soon as I ...

DANI. Now.

NOLA. The big man, he ...

DANI. I'm paid to hurt people, you understand.

(A moment. NOLA sweeps.)

DANI. Tiger. You are drivin' me nuts.

TIGER. I like lookin' in lockers.

DANI. How's that rat doin'?

TIGER. Chihuahua. Bes' goddamn roommate I ever had.

DANI. Bigman says you bring her in here he's gonna eat her.

TIGER. Be the last bite he ever takes. She don't like that Motel 6. Got a nosebleed. (*SHE takes her out.*)

DANI. You get any sleep?

TIGER. Not a hell of a lot.

DANI. Eighth graders. They oughta electrocute 'em, not put 'em in a motel. Where's Bigman?

TIGER. On a pay phone.

DANI. Where's his brother, Eddie the asshole?

TIGER. Cruiserweight Champion of America?

DANI. Ain't that a bitch? Crowd loves them cruiserweights. I gotta see a gynecologist.

TIGER. Oughta cut down to two room-clerks a week.

NOLA. Want me to wipe out some lockers?

DANI. Yeah. (*To Tiger.*) Where else am I gonna find a man by the time the bus gets in?

TIGER. Forget it.

DANI. I like to stay in working order.

TIGER. (*Short laugh.*) I'd rather rust.

DANI. There's a dead rat in the showers.

NOLA. Showers don't work anyway.

DANI. Great. You want the other half of this cardboard burrito?

TIGER. (*Takes it.*) Sure. What town are we in? (*Puts her dog back in the cat case.*)

DANI. Deepest Tennessee.

TIGER. No, really, what town?

DANI. Hey, Tiger, I really *don't* know. What town were we in yesterday?

NOLA. Cementville. You're in Cementville, Tennessee.

(DANI and TIGER snort.)

DANI. I'm in Cementville, Tennessee, with the All American Wrestling Federation Shower of Stars Tour. (*To Tiger.*) You got aspirin?

NOLA. How many stars?

TIGER. What was that, kid? *(Getting the aspirin.)*

NOLA. How many stars we in for tonight?

DANI. Well, kid, that's somethin' the rubes never know. You got five bucks?

TIGER. Hey.

DANI. This is a *fan,* Tiger. What separates the fans from the rubes is inside dope. You a fan, Nola?

NOLA. Yes ma'am.

DANI. You got five bucks?

NOLA. I got twenty bucks.

TIGER. Don't let her hustle you.

DANI. Five bucks I answer three questions. (*Takes the aspirin without water.)*

TIGER. I'm going for the big man. (*Stops by Nola. Gives money.*) This is for the beer. The buck's a tip. Keep an eye on that case. (*SHE exits.*)

DANI. She got a steel plate in her head.

NOLA. No.

DANI. Yeah. I fucked Tom Cruise.

NOLA. Yeah?

DANI. Yeah.

(NOLA pulls out her money, peels off a five, holds it out. DANI takes it.)

DANI. O.K. The question was how many stars? You got a cigarette?

NOLA. Sure.

DANI. Cementville, Tennessee, huh? (*NOLA nods.*) You ever heard of Madison Square Garden? (*NOLA shakes her head "no."*) Well, I played there and now I'm playin' here.

NOLA. Wow!

DANI. O.K., we got the main event, right? Irish Bob McCarthy vs. Stosha "The Wild Man" Oronovsky.

NOLA. Whew!

DANI. That's Bigman doin' the Irish an his brother Eddie the asshole doin' the Ruskie. They fought for the championship eighty-three times this year.

NOLA. (*Shocked.*) Brothers?

DANI. Yeah.

NOLA. Irish Bob?

DANI. Well, he ain't Irish and he ain't Bob, an he owes me four weeks salary, the scumbag. Anyway, there's those two plus me, Tiger, Netty and Angelessa. O.K. We open up with me wrestlin' Tiger. Then Netty wrestles Angelessa. Then Tiger wrestles Angelessa masked. On like that 'til the combinations run out. Girls do tag team, then Bigman an the asshole do the Cruiserweight Championship, an we grab some showers an go out an get wasted.

NOLA. (*A pause.*) Just six stars?

DANI. Yeah, right.

NOLA. Doin' the whole thing?

DANI. Six, yeah.

NOLA. Who's the woman in the iron mask?

DANI. Sometimes Angelessa, sometimes me.

NOLA. Shoot. She was my favorite an she ain't even a person.

DANI. It's a bitch, ain't it? You got one more question for the five bucks.

NOLA and DANI. How can I get started in professional wrestling?

DANI. One: it's major shit work for bad pay. Two: gives you foot fungus. Three: wrestlers got an attitude an bad knees. Now get the hell out of here, I'm tired of you.

NOLA. O.K.

(As SHE starts to leave, NETTY, a motherly woman in her forties, enters with ANGELESSA, a powerful black wrestler in her late twenties dressed in a sweatsuit with a college name and "Property of the Athletic Dept." emblazoned on it. SHE is carrying a large duffel bag. SHE wears a Walkman.)

NETTY. Oh my God, did we have a good, good, good, good dinner. Country cookin'. Green beans, darlin', so much good bacon fat they kep' on slippin' out of my mouth onto the floor. Hi, Dani. (*To Nola.*) Who's this pretty thing?

NOLA. Hey.

DANI. Helpin' clean up this pigsty.

NETTY. (*Cheerful.*) Ooooooo, it's nasty, isn't it. What's your name, darlin'?

NOLA. Nola.

NETTY. Uh-huh, that's a pretty name. You straight or gay, honey?

NOLA. Huh?

NETTY. Boys or girls?

(NOLA stares at her nonplussed.)

NETTY. Well, never mind, you'll get it figured out. You seen Eddie?

DANI. Haven't seen him.

NETTY. Well, I'm worried about that vicious ol' fart. No answer in his room.

DANI. Forgot to brush his teeth an died of the smell.

NETTY. Oh, now. He's our meal ticket an we got to worry over him. (*To Nola.*) Darlin', you gonna get us a bench to sit down on? I'm a big ol' fat lady, I got to have me a bench. Y'all want some Black Jack chewin' gum? Angelessa? *(To Dani.)* Angelessa ain't talkin', she's in a depression.

DANI. She's always in a depression.

NETTY. Oh, she is not. (*To Nola.*) Scoot. Shoo. You help us out now, O.K.?

(NOLA exits. NETTY speaks loudly because of Lessa's walkman.)

DANI. What happened to your eye?

LESSA. Somebody messed with me.

NETTY. You smile, the ol' world smiles with you.

LESSA. I got about two hundred aggravated reasons to kill people. You smile.

DANI. (*Pushing Lessa's duffel bag with her foot.*) Goin' somewhere?

LESSA. Get your foot off my bag.

DANI. You cop a fade, you owe me fifteen bucks.

NETTY. You know, you got me thinkin' now ... what if the asshole O.D.'s in his room? I mean, he's a freebaser, right? Wasn't he freebasin'? He was. Shoot. That just about gets me worried.

DANI. Bigman said he was clean.

NETTY. Well, they're brothers, honey. They got to speak well of each other.

(NOLA enters dragging two benches.)

NETTY. You are a dreamboat, sweetie. That's a real nice bench. Have yourself some Black Jack Gum, it's refreshin'.

(NOLA takes a piece.)

NETTY. (*To Nola.*) You seen the costume trunks, darlin'? (*To Dani.*) Didn't I just see them in the hall?

(LESSA nods, NETTY speaks to Nola.)

NETTY. You wanta drag those trunks on in here, honey? See, I'm a fat lady an I got a bad back.

(NOLA goes to do her bidding. TIGER re-enters.)

NETTY. Tiger, which way I go for the coin telephone?

TIGER. Bigman's on it.

NETTY. Only one?

TIGER. Only one I saw.

NETTY. You seen the asshole?

TIGER. Not since I screwed him.

NETTY. You did not?

TIGER. Two years ago.

NETTY. You saw him on the bus last night.

TIGER. I see him, but I don' *see* him. You know what I mean?

(NOLA drags a costume trunk into the room. LESSA takes off her walkman. TIGER reads her comic.)

NETTY. Well, nobody has seen him and that's what I'm talking about. You think I should get Bigman?

LESSA. (*Gets down to do stretching exercises.)* He usually on time.

DANI. Oooooo, you gettin' on that floor?

TIGER. There's bad shit on that floor, Lessa.

LESSA. I got to stretch.

DANI. Well, I'm not stretchin' on that floor.

LESSA. You never did.

DANI. Now don't get on my back, Lessa. I got infected ovaries. (*DANI lights up a cigarette.*)

NETTY. Well, you poor thing. (*NOLA drags in a second trunk.*) Ain't that nice? You know we gonna be in bed without a vibrator the asshole don't show up.

TIGER. (*A crooked grin.*) Nice talk, Mama.

NETTY. Them fans wanna see them Champion Cruiserweights.

TIGER. (*To Nola.*) Wanna pull that thing over here? (*TIGER gets their first aid kit, a red fishing tackle box, out of the trunk.*)

NETTY. The rubes be wantin' their money back, we be in bed without a vibrator.

LESSA. Don't call 'em rubes.

NETTY. The fans ...

LESSA. That's right.

DANI. They're rubes.

LESSA. Fans!

NETTY. Now you two, be nice.

NOLA. 'Scuse me.

NETTY. What's that, darlin'?

NOLA. (*To Tiger.*) I'm goin' for the beer.

LESSA. (*From the floor.*) No rat dogs or alcohol in the dressin' room.

TIGER. The dog goes where I go. I'm in Cementville, Tennessee. I got bad ribs, dog's got a nosebleed, I ain't been paid an I'm gettin' a six-pack. (*TIGER takes a large pill bottle out of the first aid box and swallows several, dry.*)

DANI. (*To Lessa.*) How come you carryin' your bag?

LESSA. Thought I'd let you do my laundry.

NETTY. See now, we're gettin' bad tempered 'cause of this money thing. I knew it.

DANI. Damn straight.

NETTY. So, I think Bigman …

DANI. I say we get cash before the show.

LESSA. An don't call it a show.

DANI. Lessa, you a real pain in the ass when you're depressed.

LESSA. I'm an athlete. I don't do a show.

DANI. O.K. I say we get cash before we do tonight's Olympics.

TIGER. He ain't gonna pay us before the show.

DANI. Well, if the asshole overdosed he ain't gonna pay us afterwards.

NETTY. Now, I think y'all ought to have a stick of Black Jack Gum ...

DANI. I'm just tired of his kickin' our butts all over the lot.

LESSA. Kept you off the street for three year.

DANI. I told you I don't like that.

NETTY. Well now, Bigman, he got various traits …

TIGER. No kiddin'.

NETTY. There's good an bad …

DANI. I'm talkin' about …

NETTY. … Take into consideration …

DANI. Paychecks!

NETTY. … Nobody here …

DANI. Lessa?

NETTY. … Starvin' to death.

DANI. Four weeks, right Lessa? (*LESSA doesn't answer.*) Four weeks, right? (*LESSA keeps warming up.*) You didn't get a paycheck, right?

LESSA. I'm into my warm-up, O.K.? Gettin' my game face together, you dig? I like to keep my mind in the ring.

DANI. You better not have got a paycheck, Lessa. I don't care what Olympics you was in, you better not a got a paycheck.

LESSA. I had a paycheck, you'd be lookin' at air.

NETTY. All I'm sayin' is I'm worried about Eddie.

TIGER. Eddie?

DANI. The asshole.

TIGER. His name's Eddie?

DANI. I thought you screwed him?

TIGER. Yeah, I screwed him but I always called him asshole.

LESSA. (*A grin.*) You kiddin'?

TIGER. Seemed to energize him.

(THEY laugh.)

NETTY. 'Cause if he's hurt or sick or somethin', well...

TIGER and LESSA. "We're just in bed without a vibrator."

(THEY laugh.)

DANI. O.K., but I got financial obligations.

LESSA. Still payin' your pimp?

(DANI turns, infuriated. TIGER steps between Dani and Lessa.)

TIGER. Enough, O.K. Jesus, I hate women.

NETTY. Must be a full moon, I swear. (*NETTY goes about taping a mirror to the front of the locker she has chosen.*)

TIGER. Let's just get the card on an get us out of this pisshole.

DANI. Easy for you to say.

TIGER. (*Points to the dog.*) Gotta get her to a vet an get me some orthopedics, O.K.? An that sure as hell ain't here.

NOLA. (*Enters.*) Six-pack. Had to go a distance.

TIGER. (*To Lessa and Dani.*) Everybody cool?

NOLA. Wasn't hardly nuthin' open. Corona, O.K.?

TIGER. Corona? Damn. That ain't that Japanese stuff, is it?

NETTY. Ooooo, Corona, that's good.

TIGER. 'Cause they put sugar in that shit, it's nasty.

NETTY. Noooo, honey, ol' Mexico. Yes ma'am. I had some good times on that beer.

(TIGER uncaps the beer with her teeth.)

DANI. Now we got to hear about the Jai Lai player's wife.

NETTY. She had three breasts, and they were perfectly formed.

(BIGMAN enters. HE wears a green polyester suit. HE looks like a wrestler.)

BIGMAN. (*Taking over as is his want.*) O.K., ladies, we got to have a little pow-wow here.

NETTY. You havin' a hard day, honey? (*SHE pats his shoulder.*)

BIGMAN. (*Seeing the case. To Tiger.*) You got that frog-dog in here?

NETTY. (*To Nola.*) You want to get us some washin' water, darlin'?

BIGMAN. Goddamit, Tiger, hand it over.

TIGER. (*Low, eyes burning.*) You would regret touchin' this dog.

BIGMAN. (*Draws back.*) Hotel called, Tiger. Seems you forgot to pay a check in the coffee shop.

TIGER. The milk was sour, the roast beef was green, and the toast was wet.

BIGMAN. We got to be good citizens, dammit.

TIGER. I ate that sandwich, I'd be a dead citizen.

BIGMAN. Pay the friggin' bill, alright?

DANI. What she 'sposed to pay for it with?

BIGMAN. Look, I got a lot of problems, I don't wanta hear this minute shit.

DANI. Don't sweat the small stuff, right?

BIGMAN. Yeah, I ...

DANI. Get to the heart of the problem.

BIGMAN. Tell me about it.

DANI. Paychecks.

(BIGMAN, as if by reflex, hits her with his open hand across the head. Not on the face but above the ear.)

TIGER. (*Knowing what's coming, leans her head against a locker.*) Damn.

DANI. You hit me, Bigman.

BIGMAN. No, I didn't.

DANI. You hit me in the head.

BIGMAN. (*To the rest.*) Sit down and listen up.

DANI. Nobody crosses that line. I don't take that from no fuckin' nobody. You hear me?

LESSA. Chill out.

DANI. (*To Lessa.*) Butt out.

(TIGER sings a couple of snatches of "Me and My Shadow.")

BIGMAN. Hey.

DANI. Hey, what?

BIGMAN. I didn't hit you.

DANI. Yeah?

BIGMAN. (*To the others.*) You hear this?

DANI. (*To the others.*) He hit me.

BIGMAN. You ever have a coach, Dani?

DANI. Get outta here.

BIGMAN. Football? Basketball? Any contact sport?

DANI. What the hell does that have to do with …

BIGMAN. You ever played a fuckin' sport you'd know what a coach was.

DANI. You hit me!

BIGMAN. I cuffed you.

DANI. Yeah, so?

BIGMAN. So the cuff is how the coach gets the athlete's attention. The cuff says wake up you are being communicated with with information.

DANI. The information is …

BIGMAN. Hold it …

DANI. You owe me four weeks' salary.

(HE cuffs her again. SHE goes after him and after a brief scuffle is subdued and held by TIGER and NETTY.)

DANI. Touch me again I'll tear your hand off.

BIGMAN. I got no time for this.

LESSA. Can I ask you a question?

BIGMAN. In a minute. Dani, Dani, your problem is inappropriate behavior. Like you don't pee in a blender.

DANI. (*To Tiger and Netty.*) Let go of me.

BIGMAN. An athlete lives physical, focused, physical. Your sprinter …

DANI. Off me!

BIGMAN. Your sprinter, short distance, waiting for the start, Chicago could fall down they don't hear it. You want to communicate mentally with an athlete ... (*HE touches her shoulder.*)

DANI. Don't touch me ...

BIGMAN. ... You gotta cuff 'em. That's all I'm sayin'. It's like an alarm bell, an idea is coming. (*HE notices his suit.*) Look at that? You got oil or some crap on my jacket. For *this* I *should* hit you. Jeez. Looka this! I cuff you like a coach. I never hit you. Is that clear?

(DANI walks over and hits the locker.)

BIGMAN. Is that clear?

(SHE hits it again.)

BIGMAN. Is that clear?

DANI. Yeah, it's clear.

BIGMAN. Good! (*To Lessa. NOLA enters with bucket of water.*) What's your question?

LESSA. We gonna wrestle?

BIGMAN. O.K., listen up. What is that, beer? (*No reaction.*) Is that a beer I see before me? What's my position on beer in the dressing room?

LESSA. No beer.

BIGMAN. That's right. Whose beer is this?

TIGER. My beer.

BIGMAN. O.K., I'm makin' an exception; gimme a beer.

(TIGER tosses him one.)

NETTY. (*Patting her.*) You doin' real good.

(NOLA exits.)

BIGMAN. What is this, Bulgarian beer? Jeeminy. You don't buy American and you piss about the country goin' down the tubes. *(HE takes a hit.)* Not bad.

NETTY. (*To Dani.*) Forget it.

DANI. (*Calmer, but still pissed.*) You forget it.

BIGMAN. O.K., you got your ears on? Hey, Lessa. *(SHE still stretches.)* Lessa. Jeez. Take a break, O.K.? (*More beer.*) O.K., you're all like family. You know that. You tour with me, you're family.

NETTY. O.K.

BIGMAN. O.K., right. We got a situation here.

(NOLA starts pulling in a dressing room unit with two mirrors surrounded by lights. It rolls.)

BIGMAN. Hey! You?

NOLA. Yo.

BIGMAN. Not now.

NOLA. You said.

BIGMAN. Not now. Read my lips.

(NOLA pulls it back out.)

BIGMAN. O.K., we got a situation. Now, we're in … where are we?

TIGER. Tennessee.

BIGMAN. I know we're in Tennessee. What am I, a moron? O.K., where in Tennessee?

TIGER. Cementville.

BIGMAN. O.K., Cementville. A good wrestlin' town. They had Wednesday night fights here ... years, O.K., a town promoted by Bill Walla, O.K.? He don't take care of business, I get us the date. The strong survive, right?

NETTY. That's right.

BIGMAN. Right. O.K. We do big, or even we do good, I get his other Tennessee dates. See the picture? Maybe next year we take all his dates get rich. You followin' me? O.K. We got a situation. My brother. (*HE takes off his hat.*) An all-star. A man put six years in the big time ... World Wrestling Federation ... A man puts butts in the seats, a draw, in other words. A headliner ...

(DANI has put up her hand.)

BIGMAN. What?

DANI. I gotta go potty.

BIGMAN. No.

DANI. No?

BIGMAN. Later.

DANI. Later what? I gotta go.

BIGMAN. Dani. The Gettysburg Address, Pearl Harbor there are times you don't go potty.

LESSA. Bigman?

BIGMAN. Yeah, what?

LESSA. They got no fights in here Wednesday nights.

BIGMAN. So?

LESSA. You said ...

BIGMAN. I said in the town. Hertzburger Arena.

DANI. Yeah? So why aren't we there?

BIGMAN. 'Cause they bumped Billy Walla for a fuckin' ice show.

DANI. So you book the Hilton here?

BIGMAN. Hey, this is a famous fight joint. Jake Lamotta, Ezzard Charles.

DANI. So what are they, cavemen?

BIGMAN. Willie Pep, Kid Gavilan, Archie Moore. This here is a place for worship. Gods, I'm not exaggeratin', gods have spilled blood here.

DANI. (*Wrinklin' her nose.*) And apparently piss.

(TIGER laughs.)

BIGMAN. Knock that off. Hey, Dani. (*HE ticks the following off on his fingers.*) Who the hell were you? Who the hell are you? And who the fuck are you gonna be when I dump you? (*There is silence in the room.*) We make the date work, next time we're in the Hertzberger Arena. (*HE looks at his watch.*) What am I talking here? I'm bleedin' time here. My brother … (*HE pauses, a strange look on his face.*) My brother is indisposed.

NETTY. I knew it.

LESSA. Damn shame.

DANI. Whatsa matter he can't fight drunk?

(In one move, BIGMAN reaches down and puts Dani up against the lockers. WOMEN scatter.)

TIGER .Whoa!

NETTY. Bigman!

(There is a frozen moment. Then, strangely, BIGMAN puts both fists to his forehead and sobs.)

BIGMAN. Oh man. Oh man.

NETTY. Hey, baby …

TIGER. O.K., Dani?

BIGMAN. That man …

NETTY. Come on, honey.

BIGMAN. Oh man.

NETTY. Sit down, darlin' …

TIGER. Take a load off, Bigman.

BIGMAN. It's O.K.

NETTY. Take a hit on the beer.

TIGER. You want a shot?

BIGMAN. Gimme room … back off.

TIGER. (*To Lessa.*) Inside my bag there, half pint …

LESSA. Not me.

TIGER. (*To Netty.*) Wild Turkey.

NETTY. One-half pint.

BIGMAN. I'm O.K., get the hell off me. (*HE stands up.*)

LESSA. (*To Dani.*) You O.K.?

NETTY. There.

TIGER. (*Bringing him the almost empty half pint.*) Try this.

BIGMAN. I'm in fuckin' AA, Tiger.

TIGER. You was drinkin' beer.

BIGMAN. Beer ain't booze. You don't hand a half pint to a man in AA.

TIGER. My mistake. (*Takes bottle.*)

BIGMAN. Have a little Goddamned consideration.

NETTY. Well, she's sorry. She is. Now you sit down an drink your beer.

BIGMAN. This ain't booze. They give this to nursin' mothers.

NOLA. (*Enters dragging the makeup mirrors.*) Comin' through.

BIGMAN. Hey!

NOLA. Yeah?

BIGMAN. I said when I said.

NOLA. You said fifteen minutes.

BIGMAN. What are you? Hearin' things? Take it out in the hall. Smoke a joint. I'll call you.

(NOLA drags the mirrors back out.)

BIGMAN. (*Getting emotional again.*) Jesus, Eddie, I don't know …

NETTY. Easy, big fella.

BIGMAN. My own brother …

NETTY. He's not dead is he, darlin'?

BIGMAN. Some bitch … I got one hundred bucks … no questions … anybody knows who was in his room last night.

(Silence. LESSA turns back to her locker.)

BIGMAN. Lessa?

DANI. Some escort whore.

BIGMAN. You saw?

DANI. A local. Blond wig.

BIGMAN. Where?

DANI. Saw her in the hallway, from the back.
BIGMAN. Yeah?
DANI. So?
BIGMAN. With him?
DANI. Yeah, he was tanked.
BIGMAN. I find her, she's dead. I find her I cut off her tits. I pull her inside out by her tongue. This is Eddie, my brother. Blood of my blood. (*HE pounds his chest.*) I'm very full.
NETTY. Of course you are.
BIGMAN. I got feelings up to here.
DANI. O.K.
NETTY. Strong feelin's.
BIGMAN. Yeah.

(A pause.)

TIGER. We cancel?
BIGMAN. No, we don't cancel! Whatta ya mean cancel? I'm like Jackie-Fuckin'-Kennedy. I'm a professional.
LESSA. Let me wrestle you.
BIGMAN. Get outta here.
LESSA. Bikini. I'll do it in a bikini.
BIGMAN. Get outta here.
LESSA. I'll do it straight.

(A pause.)

BIGMAN. Straight?
LESSA. Real.
BIGMAN. Real? What are you, a brain transplant?

LESSA. I bench press 300. I'm an Olympic athlete.

DANI. Yeah, 19th in the shot put.

LESSA. (*To Dani.*) Yeah, well, I was there. Where were you?

BIGMAN. Ladies, demeanor, O.K.?

DANI. I just saved your ass, Lessa ...

BIGMAN. Hey! O.K. Lessa. Number one, "real" looks like nuthin'. You seen "real" wrestlin'? The fans would rather watch paint dry. You know who comes to watch "real"? Mothers, mothers come to watch. And while they watch they knit. You're fuckin' screwy, O.K.? Number two, I win, who cares, you win, listen, you think two thousand morons in tractor hats wanna see a black chick ice the Cruiserweight contender? What, is this whole business lost on you? I got a brother in the hospital, unconscious. I don't have time for this.

TIGER. So we cancel, right?

BIGMAN. What'd I tell you?

NETTY. You said no.

BIGMAN. What is a promoter?

DANI. Don't ask.

BIGMAN. I'm serious. C'mon. What's a promoter?

TIGER. A guy with front money?

BIGMAN. No.

NETTY. Makes arrangements?

BIGMAN. No.

DANI. Fucks other people with promises?

BIGMAN. He's like a farmer ...

TIGER. Get outta here.

BIGMAN. From piss he makes peaches.

NETTY. This is a nice thought.

BIGMAN. Thank you. No Eddie. This is like a huge, monster problem. Do we fold? No. I got responsibilities to my girls. I'm like your father.

DANI. Hand me that other beer, will ya?

BIGMAN. I get on the phone, I get a replacement.

TIGER. Yeah?

BIGMAN. But not on a plateau, you know? I see in the problem an opportunity. I make a big move and get a big payoff. So who, who do I get?

DANI. Gorgeous fuckin' George comes back from the dead.

BIGMAN. The Knockout Sisters.

NETTY. You're kiddin'?

TIGER. The blondes?

BIGMAN. *60 Minutes.* Connie Chung Saturday Night. Presenters on the goddamned Grammies!

TIGER. (*To Bigman.*) The blondes with tits?

(BIGMAN nods, a long pause.)

LESSA. They are coming here?

BIGMAN. Bingo.

(Pause.)

LESSA. Didn't they get picked up in a drug raid screwin' the L.A. mayor?

BIGMAN. Yeah, briefly, but, *People* Magazine, *National Enquirer* ...

DANI. Banned from wrestlin' for life?

BIGMAN. Hey, people forgive.

LESSA. They got film on them doin' crack.

BIGMAN. So?

DANI. *Screw Magazine* has them on the cover makin' a sandwich with the mayor.

BIGMAN. It's publicity.

LESSA. They barred for life.

BIGMAN. From W.W.F., from A.W.P. These are giants, these are corporations. I'm an independent.

TIGER. Hey, Bigman, they are in the slammer.

BIGMAN. Nah.

TIGER. Get your money out man, they are doing time.

BIGMAN. (*Unfolding a newspaper.*) What does this say?

NETTY. "The Knockout Sisters, free at last and home with Mama."

BIGMAN. Cairo, Tennessee. The mother lives in Cairo, Tennessee. So, I'm a genius or I'm a genius? Peaches from piss, right?

(The WOMEN pass the paper around.)

TIGER. You pulled that off?

BIGMAN. One phone call. Twenty-five cents.

DANI. Get outta here?

BIGMAN. (*To Dani.*) Tell me I'm good.

DANI. You're an animal.

BIGMAN. Tell me I'm good.

(A pause.)

DANI. You're good.

BIGMAN. You betcher ass. I am *good.*

TIGER. They travelin' with us?

BIGMAN. (*Nods yes.*) We treat 'em right.

DANI. What're you payin' 'em?

BIGMAN. O.K., I got a lot to do.

DANI. I don't get a check tonight, Bigman, I'm walkin'.

LESSA. I'm gettin' a check *and* I'm walkin'.

BIGMAN. Ladies, don't promise nuthin' you can't deliver. O.K. I'm makin' out a card. The sisters supposed to drive up here in ten minutes. First two prelims same as always. Get dressed. (*Starts for the door. Turns. Exuberantly throws his fist in the air.*) Yes! (*Does a little end-zone dance Spikes his hat.*) Touchdown! (*Picks it up.*) You wanta see a promoter, ladies? Bigman, he says, he does, it's done. Believe it! (*HE exits. There is a pause.*)

TIGER. (*To Lessa.*) How much support wrap you got?

LESSA. Six-foot roll.

TIGER. I'll buy it off you.

LESSA. You can have it.

(The WOMEN begin to put necessaries from their bags into lockers.)

DANI. He's got to pay 'em what?

NETTY. Mucho dinero.

DANI. Man, it boils me!

LESSA. They get paid, we get paid.

NOLA. (*Enters with makeup tables.*) Comin' through.

TIGER. (*Pulling a comic book out of her bag to read.*) You seen their act?

DANI. Nothin', their act is nothin'.

LESSA. No moves, no skills.

NETTY. Y'all foolin' yourselves.

LESSA. Yeah?

NETTY. They got "it."

LESSA. They a couple crack-head whores. I'm embarrassed to be in the same locker room with 'em.

DANI. Stand around …

LESSA. Stan' around. Lie around. Hell, I hear they was doin' some Danish sex show and Man Mountain Montgomery zipped up his fly an discovered 'em. You know what their finishin' hold is? The Va-Va-Voom—it's a bump-and-grind makes their opponents faint.

(NOLA plugs in makeup table lights.)

TIGER. What the hell is that?

NOLA. Dressin' table.

DANI. Where'd you get it?

NOLA. Rosemary Clooney's dressin' room.

TIGER. Say what?

NOLA. There's this room, see. Little room. Got about two inches of water on the floor an the lights don't work. Got a poster for Rosemary Clooney on the door an dead roses inside.

NETTY. Rosemary Clooney?

TIGER. Ol' time country singer, died when her plane hit a mountain.

LESSA. Yeah, right.

DANI. Some real singer played this dump?

NOLA. She looked real pretty on the poster.

TIGER. Started out singin' back-up for Chubby Checker.

NETTY. Oh, that one.

DANI. Well, who you think ol' Rosemary's dressin' table is for?

LESSA. He's givin' those bitches a dressin' table?

NETTY. Now y'all listen here now …

DANI. I don't …

NETTY. Dani …

DANI. Want to damn well …

NETTY. Mark my …

DANI. Hear it.

NETTY. I'm just an old Alabama waitress now but I'm makin' more wrasslin' three nights a week …

TIGER. When we're lucky …

NETTY. … than I did slingin' hash in seven, and I ain't the only one.

DANI. (*To Tiger.*) She's goin' now.

NETTY. Owe ol' Bigman for gettin' into show business …

TIGER. Jesus.

NETTY. … an havin' us a better life, praise the Lord. (*A moment.*) Just thought I'd speak up. People who ain't stayin' should get goin', and people who are stayin' should get dressed.

(A pause.)

NOLA. I saw 'em on television.

NETTY. (*To the wrestlers.*) Them girls is an *attraction.* Now let's *get down.* (*SHE begins to tape herself up for the fight.*)

NOLA. There's a tall one an a short one an the short one is mean an sneaky an, you know, hateful, an the tall one smiles an does, like, you know, dance steps an fluffs out her hair an has a pet tarantula.

DANI. (*Cold.*) Sounds great.

NOLA. An they're sexy as all hell with kinda Cher costumes, an they come on to the fans who go like boogaloo and love 'em.

LESSA. What's your name, girl?

NOLA. Nola.

LESSA. O.K., Nola, shut the fuck up.

NOLA. Sorry.

NETTY. Got me a bruise shape of an elephant.

LESSA. Hey, Netty, I'm a professional, you know? I got pride in my work. I do hard, dangerous stuff. I don't get hurt an nobody in the ring with me gets hurt. Now you put a couple showgirls in with me they gonna spend a lotta time on their ass. They screw with my timing I'm gonna take 'em out.

DANI. Well, I don't really think you got a problem.

LESSA. Yeah, why is that?

DANI. 'Cause you ain't gonna be in the ring with 'em.

LESSA. They gonna fight Bigman for the Cruiserweight championship?

DANI. It's Tiger and me do the semi-final so it's Tiger and me move up.

LESSA. Tiger ain't got the moves, she on the injured list, plus they gonna be lookin' for bad guys, O.K.? An' you our little heroine.

DANI. Get it, I make fifty more a week. I'm on the poster. I got top girl's billing an do the top girl's fight.

LESSA. Yeah, well, you watch how it goes down.

DANI. I got the *contract*!

NETTY. (*To Tiger.*) How you feelin', honey?

TIGER. I feel like shit.

LESSA. All bets is off around here, you mark my words.

TIGER. Stifferen' hell an got about a third mobility.

DANI. You better pull in your horns, Lessa. You gonna need a friend with Bigman.

LESSA. What's that sposed to mean?

DANI. You know just what I mean, baby. Go on, tell me you don't.

LESSA. Screw you. (*Puts her walkman back on.*)

DANI. Yeah, right. (*Goes to trunk.*) You want your stuff, Netty?

NETTY. I want romance.

(DANI hands her a costume from the trunk. NETTY starts to dress as "Pajama Mama.")

DANI. Romance on the road. You want to suit up, Tiger?

TIGER. I want good drugs, a beach, an a hunnert comic books.

(DANI hands her a costume. TIGER begins to dress as "Bloody Mary"—a red leotard with metal studding.)

DANI. (*Tapes a mirror to her mirror.*) I want to win me a cruise vacation an marry any Arab we ain't shot. (*To Nola.*) Whatta you want, kid?

NOLA. I want to wrestle.

DANI. Yeah, it's a fuckin' paradise to be in wrestlin', kid. Travel opportunities, glamorous companions, luxurious surroundings, big money an the opportunity to meet crack-heads who went down on the mayor of L.A. (*SHE ruffles Nola's hair. DANI begins to dress as Tarzana, Queen of the Jungle.*)

NETTY. *(To Nola.)* I done twenty-six different jobs.

DANI. Oh man ...

NETTY. I done dry cleanin', road work, cannin' line, store clerk, bartender,

NETTY.	LESSA.
typewriter repair, phone company, re-solin', slaughterhouse, garbageman, dock loader ... hotel maid, post office, fire fightin' ... fast food, shirt factory, sewer sweep.	Which trunk is my stuff in? TIGER. Over there.

NETTY. 'Bout as close to a movie star I'm gettin'.

NOLA. I know the holds ...

(LESSA begins to dress as "Black Lightning," a super hero outfit with a lightning logo across the front.)

NETTY. Uh-huh. That's good, honey.

NOLA. Backbreaker, pretzel, rope loop, double camel. I know all the holds.

NETTY. Well, sure, the holds is your basic ... but you got your showmanship an your crowd work, see ... (*NETTY has finished dressing in a voluminous pair of striped men's pajamas.*)

NOLA. Boy, look at that! What you call that?

NETTY. Pajama Mama.

TIGER, DANI, LESSA. She puts 'em to sleep! (*TIGER begins to lace on boots.*)

NETTY. Say, you want to come up to the hotel after the show…

DANI. She'll show you a few holds ain't on your list.

NETTY. Now, that ain't nice.

DANI. True though.

NETTY. I don't work your side of the street, you oughta give me room.

DANI. Hell, there's enough hotel clerks for everybody. (*SHE starts to do her makeup.*)

NOLA. Sure.

NETTY. What's that, honey?

NOLA. I'd like to.

NETTY. Uh-huh.

NOLA. Get a few tips.

NETTY. Uh-huh. Well, O.K. then.

DANI. (*To Netty but half amused.*) Surgeon General oughta stick a message on your pussy.

NETTY. Now just knock that off.

(LESSA, with her basic fight costume on, kneels briefly and bows her head. NETTY begins to lace on boots.)

DANI. Will you stop prayin', Lessa, I can't stand that!

LESSA. (*Rising and looking in the Knockout Sisters' mirror.*) How we supposed to do if the bitches got the only mirror?

TIGER. What the hell happened to Eddie? (*A pause.*) We talkin' about this, we talkin' about that, how come the man ain't wrestlin'? (*No answer.*) Yeah, sure he's an asshole, but he's *our* asshole.

NETTY. Well, you know Eddie ...

TIGER. Yeah, I know Eddie ... probably dropped some laced meth.

NETTY. Well, now, Eddie'd been saying he was clean.

DANI. Maybe you heard somethin', huh, Lessa? (*No response.*)

NETTY. He's been havin' that little numbness in his left hand.

TIGER. I seen Eddie wrestle real hurt. I seen him wrestle through a hamstring.

NETTY. Heart trouble?

TIGER. Bigman would have said.

LESSA. Somebody bit his dick off.

DANI.Yeah, sure.

LESSA. I'm tellin' you.

DANI. Bullshit.

LESSA. O.K. They didn't bite his dick off.

TIGER. You kiddin' or what?

LESSA. Two AM. There's this screamin', Eddie's on the floor outside his room ...

NETTY. Who would do a thing like that?

DANI. I would but you'd probably get food poisoning.

(TIGER gives her the thumbs up sign.)

NETTY. (*To Lessa.*) He was naked in the hallway?

LESSA. Pretty ugly, thrashing around, yellin'. I called the paramedics. Did a tourniquet.

NETTY. (*Horrified.*) You did a tourniquet?

LESSA. Used some dental floss. Shut down the blood but he fainted.

TIGER. Jesus!

LESSA. You said he was with some whore, huh, Dani?

DANI. Yeah, he was with some whore.

NETTY. I told that man, I told him stop messin' with strange all the time. God, how much got bit off?

LESSA. I forgot my ruler, O.K.?

NETTY. Shoot *I'd* service him he wasn't so mean.

TIGER. Jesus, Netty!

NETTY. Well, that poor man didn't have a thing in the world but that dick and now it's bit off.

TIGER. Maybe they can sew it back on. They tell you now you get a finger cut off in a lawn mower you wrap it up in a Kleenex bring it down to the hospital.

DANI. They wrap his dick in a Kleenex, Lessa?

LESSA. Put it in a sandwich bag.

NETTY. Now there's some men you can picture without a dick but poor Eddie just isn't one of 'em.

TIGER. He didn't pay her, or what?

LESSA. Or worse.

DANI. Life's just funny in't? Here you're the one hates his ass an you're the one there to help.

NOLA. You think he can come back an wrestle without a dick?

DANI. His dick didn't work when he had it.

NETTY. Now no speakin' ill of the man when he's bad off.

DANI. I'd speak ill of him on the best day he ever had. He's a schizoid scumbag. And there isn't anybody in here

... except her ... (*Points at Nola.*) doesn't know it personal.

TIGER. Well, whoever done it put us in a hell of a fix. Now that's straight.

LESSA. Whoever done it probably had a damn good reason. An that's straight.

TIGER. (*Pulling out a tin of gourmet dog food and an opener. As SHE talks, SHE feeds her dog.*) This tour folds, we a bunch a worn out ol' bitches on the street. An if the word is some one of us chomped his member they'd hire the Hells Angels before they'd hire us. I got no skills, an armed robbery conviction, an a sick dog. Now let's kiss ass an wrestle.

NETTY. On the money. (*A moment.*) Now Eddie did say it was a whore, right?

TIGER. Far as we hear Eddie ain't said shit, an Eddie won't say shit, he'll just kill somebody.

(There is a CRASH behind the door between the lockers—the WOMEN turn.)

DANI. You hear that? That's rats. We in this dressing room with rats!

NETTY. Now take it easy, honey ...

DANI. No way. Noooooooo way.

(LESSA opens the door. A small MAN in his early forties wearing jeans, a work shirt and Vietnamese Tiger jacket is revealed nervously clutching a thick autograph book.)

DWAYNE. How you doin'?

TIGER. Son of a bitch.

DANI. You scruffy little maggot what you doin' in here?

LESSA. Step outta there, cracker.

DWAYNE. Yes ma'am. Yes ma'am. Dwayne Arthur Pardee. How you doin'?

LESSA. How'm I doin'? What're you doin'? You in the broom closet, Dwayne whatsit.

DANI. You in there lookin' for Rosemary Clooney, or what?

TIGER. (*Pulling him up in her face by the shirt front.*) You in there lookin' for poontang, Dwayne?

LESSA. You in there chokin' the turkey?

DWAYNE. No ma'am.

LESSA. No ma'am what?

DWAYNE. I ain't chokin' the turkey.

NETTY. Well, you been in there a hell of a long time, honey.

DWAYNE. Yes ma'am.

NETTY. (*Moving Tiger away from him.*) Well, you wanta tell Momma why you in there?

DWAYNE. Yes ma'am. See, I'm an autograph professional.

DANI. You a professional nutcase.

NETTY. (*To Dani.*) Now hush now. (*To Dwayne.*) You been in there a couple hours waitin' for our autograph?

DWAYNE. Well ... see ... I was in, you know ... an umm ... an this uh big fellow he uh ... uh ...

NETTY. Kind put you out?

DWAYNE. He did. He did. So I ... you know ...

NETTY. Come on back in?

DWAYNE. I did. I did. An he us ... an he uh ...

NETTY. Kinda put you back out?

TIGER. Netty, get him outta here.

NETTY. This is a fan, O.K.? This is a wrestlin' fan.

DANI. He's a fuckin' pervert.

DWAYNE. No ma'am, I'm an autograph professional. I got ... I got every famous person ... everyone been in Cementville since ... see here ... (*Opens the autograph book.*) 1972. Cass Elliott. Ol' Mama Cass. Year before she died. God bless her. See 1972. Gene Hackman. The Four Preps. Well, three of 'em. See this here this is American heroes, see, the American way right here, right here in Cementville. O.J. Simpson. See? Irene Ryan, you know, Beverly Hillbillies. Tony Boyle, United Mine Workers. See this here is goin' in a time capsule. Anita Bryant, God bless her. See here. This is my life work.

NETTY. Well, good on you.

DANI. Get him outta here.

NETTY. Now you want us to sign your book, honey, huh?

DWAYNE. Yes ma'am. I do. Yes ma'am, yes ma'am.

NETTY. Now Dwayne, you wasn't watchin' us get dressed through a crack 'er somethin' and jerkin' off in there, was you?

DWAYNE. No ma'am. No ma'am. I wouldn't do that.

NETTY. 'Cause then we'd have to kill you, Dwayne.

DWAYNE. Well, you know, the big fella ...

NETTY. You was hidin' from the big fella?

DWAYNE. Yes ma'am, I wasn't ... well, what you said.

NETTY. O.K., we'll sign your book then. (*SHE takes it.*)

DWAYNE. God bless you. You just an American Beauty Rose in my book. You American heroes, God bless yer pure hearts. You gonna be in the time capsule. You gonna be there when Jesus Christ walks again.

(During his speech, the WOMEN, even NOLA, sign his book.)

DWAYNE. You the mothers of America. Umm, one to a page, ma'am. You the heart, the red heart of us men folks. You the arms that swing the cradle. You on a pedestal, a way high pedestal to Dwayne Pardee. Yes sir. You a hot lunch when the men's in the fields. Yes sir, you may be prostitutes an wrasslers but you mean home to me.

NETTY. O.K., Dwayne, we about got this together now.

DWAYNE. You cut from the cloth of Jesus Christ's momma. Yes ma'am. An I'm talkin' for the mens now. Speakin' for your daddies.

TIGER. (*The last to sign.*) O.K., Dwayne.

DWAYNE. For your husbands and sons an I say to you: Get you home an get me some dinner, bitch …

DANI. (*Head in her hands.*) Oh man …

DWAYNE. … Goin' to town in yer red lipstick, paradin' yourself like Jezebel with a tambourine, bringin' down the temple with your lascivious hips …

LESSA. (*Moving towards him.*) Let's take a walk, dude.

DWAYNE. (*Grabbing Tiger from behind.*) Touch me, Loretta …

(SHE gives a sharp cry because of her ribs.)

DWAYNE. Touch me, rub me, take me to heaven!

(LESSA grabs him by the hair. HE lets go. SHE throws a hammerlock on him and turns him to the door.)

LESSA. Walk.

DWAYNE. My book … gimme my book …

LESSA. (*Taking him out the door.*) Move it.

DWAYNE. I'm a … ouch! … autograph professional … you hurtin' my arm …

LESSA. I'm breakin' your arm … (*And THEY are gone.*)

TIGER. … the damn ribs.

DANI. You O.K., Tiger?

TIGER. Don't touch me.

NETTY. Stand up.

TIGER. Hold on …

NETTY. Stand up, it's better, honey.

TIGER. Son-of-a-bitch … ow … leggo … damn … mother-brother-son-of-a-bitch kiss my ass dammit … (*Tiger's furious tirade finally reduces the rest to laughter.*) Hate this damn wrasslin' … ow … got up like some kinda … stupid … Goddamn ribs … shoulda torn off that autograph bastard's balls, hung 'em on a rear view like Goddamn cashmere dice … itchin' all over, fleas, head lice … get the Goddamn bubonic plague in this Goddamn shit hole … get the athletes foot … what the hell are you laughin' at, you cross-eyed, knock-kneed, piss-ant, putrid, dick-lickin', flat-chested, slung-assed nowhere broads! (*SHE starts laughing too.*) Don't make me laugh!

DANI. You aren't mad, are you, Tiger?

(More laughter.)

TIGER. Hell, no, I'm happy!

NOLA. He left his book. (*Holds up the autograph book.*)

DANI. Gimme that thing.

NOLA. Well, but it's ...

DANI. (*Taking it from her.*) I said hand it over. (*Rips out handfuls of pages, walks to door and flings them down the hall.*) Pervert!

TIGER. Son of a bitch.

DANI. You know they got celebrity insurance now. All these nutzoids trying to shoot movie stars. (*Finishing her makeup.*)

TIGER. We ain't movie stars.

DANI. You tellin' me.

NOLA. You think he was kind of crazy?

DANI. Yeah. An he ain't the worst. We the entertainment for fuckups. When you go crazy tryin' to live this life they send you over here for Wednesday night wrestlin'.

NOLA. (*Looking at the ripped-out pages.*) Who's Eugene McCarthy?

NETTY. (*To Tiger.*) Can you get up, honey?

TIGER. Yeah, I can, but not yet.

(LESSA re-enters.)

NETTY. (*To Lessa.*) O.K.?

LESSA. Yeah.

DANI. (*To Lessa.*) So?

LESSA. Said I was his Ethiopian Queen, said come over to his place he had musk oil.

DANI. What'd you do with him?

LESSA. Put him in the dumpster.

NETTY. How long you think he was in the broom closet?

LESSA. I think he grew there like a fuckin' mushroom.

NETTY. Talkin' the good book ...

LESSA. An' humpin' parking meters. Yeah, I was married to a preacher once.

NETTY. Well, now, I didn't know that.

LESSA. It ain't your job to know, is it?

TIGER. (*To Netty.*) Give me a hand up.

LESSA. 'Bout the last thing I need me is a soulmate.

DANI. No problem.

LESSA. Zip my head.

(NETTY pulls Tiger up.)

RING ANNOUNCER. (*Offstage at a distance.*)

(Ring BELL.)

Ladies and gentlemen, the all-American Wrestling Federation presents its Shower of Stars Tour.

BIGMAN. (*Enters.*) All right, lemme have your attention. *(Calls out to the hall.)* Come on in here, Mother.

(MOTHER CROCKER, a rough looking woman in her late fifties in a black church dress with a strand of

pearls. SHE smokes a cigarillo. SHE enters and appraises the room and its inhabitants.)

BIGMAN. This here is Mother Crocker, Mama and Manager for the Knockout Sisters ... step in, Mother ... she'd like to give us a little ground plan on how it's gonna come down tonight. Mother Crocker, I'd like to welcome you to the American Wrestling Federation. We got the finest up an coming girls in the sport. An I'd like to personally express my thoughts on the job you done makin' the Knockout Sisters a world-wide attraction. You done a great job. O.K., let 'er rip.

MOTHER. Pretty run-down lookin' bunch.

BIGMAN. Yeah, but wait 'til you see 'em in action!

MOTHER. Y'all are dead meat. You're a two-bit tour playin' morgue dates and you got never-was, never-will-be talent on the way down. I wouldn't be caught dead puttin' my top attraction down this pisshole but I got me a public relations problem. See, we messed up, got ourselves into politics, put a crimp in our image. Now we got to lay low, stay in shape an make a few bucks. On the upside we probably goin' to get a film deal out of that mess, we're negotiatin'. The Knockout Sisters is A-One, U.S. prime horseflesh. While we're slummin' with you girls, you're going to have ace crowds an make the only decent money you ever made in your miserable lives. While we're together your sports pimp here ... (*Indicating Bigman.*) ... gets me coffee. You understand? I say fuck a sheep, he fucks a sheep, is that clear?

BIGMAN. (*A big smile.*) She got a great sense of humor, doesn't she?

MOTHER. Now think this over. How do you think a couple small-town girls became the fourth biggest wrestling attraction in the United States of America in two years? (*SHE pauses.*) That's right. Mobbed up. Just like Sinatra. You capice? Now this wrestlin' wears out an attraction, which is why we segue into film. But meanwhile, meanwhile don't bruise the meat. You understand me? You injure, deface or otherwise crumb up the dollar value on my attraction you're going to hear some fucking Sicilian. Got it? Dottie, Dolly, get in here.

(The KNOCKOUT SISTERS, one tall, one short, both attractive in a hard way with platinum hair, little bare-shouldered mauve dresses and spike heels, enter.)

MOTHER. Say hello to the little people.
DOTTIE. I'm Dottie.
DOLLY. I'm Dolly.
MOTHER. Who are you?
DOTTIE and DOLLY. We're the Knockout Sisters.
MOTHER. (*To the room.*) Remember what I said.

BLACKOUT

END OF ACT I

ACT II

The fights are on. The first prelim is over. DANI is changing from her Tarzana costume to her Texas Gold outfit, featuring gold sequins, gold cape and a gold cowboy hat. TIGER is still basically in her Bloody Mary outfit. NETTY and ANGELESSA are upstairs working. The KNOCKOUT SISTERS in little lavender dressing kimonos are heavily into their glamour makeup trip. MOTHER is out watching the fights, and BIGMAN is ranking out Dani and Tiger for the quality of their work. DOTTIE has decorated her locker with scarves, photos, dried flowers, and Eastern wisdom.

BIGMAN. I got seven hundred rubes out there laughin' their asses off while you pattycake.

DANI. Hey, I can't touch her ribs or put her on the floor, or if I get her on the floor she can't get off the floor, so what am I supposed to do?

DOTTIE. (*Stretching and preparing.*) Money, money, money, money, money, money, money, money ...

BIGMAN.	DOTTIE.
An athlete eats pain for lunch, Tiger.	Money, money, money, money, money, money,
TIGER.	money, money, money,
Dammit, where's that whiskey?	money, money, money.

BIGMAN. (*To Dottie.*) What the hell is that?

DOTTIE. It's my warm-up.

DANI. You got seven hundred rubes, huh?

BIGMAN. Yeah, six hundred, six fifty.

DANI. Three hundred, countin' people with a brain twice.

DOTTIE. See, life is a series of circles. One circle inside the next, inside the next.

BIGMAN. (*Trying to be polite.*) Circles, uh-huh. (*To Tiger.*) Got to get the rubes *hot,* Tiger. Get 'em wild and riled. They not *smokin'*, they get pissed.

TIGER.
I don't know, Bigman.

BIGMAN.
Put 'em on the edge. Keep 'em on the edge.

DOTTIE.
Each one of us has a circle. See on that circle ... (*To Bigman.*) Excuse me, I am talkin' to you.

BIGMAN. You got a circle. We got a circle. Everybody got a circle.

DOTTIE. You got two choices—get enlightened or die.

BIGMAN. Sounds real good. (*To Tiger.*) You got to go back out there with Lessa ...

DOTTIE. Excuse me ...

BIGMAN. An *turn it on*. They gonna be walkin' out!

DOTTIE. Excuse me.

BIGMAN. What!?

DOTTIE. Now I don't like that tone. Did you hear that tone, Dolly?

DOLLY. Yeah.

DOTTIE. Sometimes a tone such as that causes me to hyperventilate, and then I jus' have to go home.

BIGMAN. Listen.

DOTTIE. Yeah.

BIGMAN. Now I'm sorry …

DOTTIE. You're sorry what?

BIGMAN. Sorry Miss Crocker.

DOLLY. That's right, pig snot.

NOLA. (*Enters with a bottle in a paper bag. To Dani.*) Shoot. I am sorry. It's kinda, well, you know, boarded up around here. Shut down. No liquor store, no nothin'. I went … finally there was, you know, this guy, you know, in a doorway, I bought this from him. (*SHE pulls out a Smirnoff bottle about a third full of brownish liquid.*)

TIGER. What the hell is that?

NOLA. Said the vodka wasn't no taste so …

DANI. That is one suspicious color.

NOLA. So he kinda flavored it with sherry.

TIGER. Hell with it. (*Takes a hit.*)

DOTTIE. Now that is disgusting.

TIGER. Yeah, it's vodka and sherry.

DANI. Nasty.

DOLLY. I don't work with drunks.

TIGER. Lady, I'm numb or I'm gone. (*A long drink.*)

DOTTIE. So that each one of us has a circle. Like this … (*Makes a circle in the air.*) A path. Call it fate. Call it what you will.

DANI. I call it bullshit.

DOTTIE. I want this woman out of the dressing room.

BIGMAN. For Christ sake, Dani, shut up. (*To Dottie.*) O.K., a circle.

DOTTIE. Yes.

BIGMAN. Of fate.

DOTTIE. Yes.

NOLA. (*To Tiger.*) I had to give him the ten. 'Cause he was like a bum—like he couldn't make change.

DOTTIE. An Dolly an me, see, we are in the circle of sex goddesses.

TIGER. I gotta get dressed, doctor my dog. (*TIGER continues dressing as Pocahontas.*)

BIGMAN. Jesus!

DOTTIE. (*Snaps Bigman with a towel.*) I am expressin' myself.

BIGMAN. (*Suppressing growing anger.*) Sex goddesses.

DOTTIE. Nefertiti, Mary Magdalene, Marilyn, Madonna and us!

BIGMAN. (*Red in the face.*) Nefertiti.

DOTTIE. That's right. We gonna get good karma, give good head, get us ace parts in the horror flicks.

DOLLY. We gonna be dismembered in a close-up the size of this fuckin' room. You watch for it!

DANI. (*In the presence of some kind of madness.*) This is *real* interestin'. (*Pulling on cowboy boots.*)

DOTTIE. We carryin' forward, along the circle, the wisdom of the forbearers … DANI. And their tits, too. Right?	RING ANNOUNCER. (*BELL sounds.*) The winner, in 17 minutes, the pleasingly fat queen of the mat … Pajama Mama! (*BELL sounds*)

DOTTIE. That too.

DANI. It's very mystical.

DOTTIE. It is. You worked with Kad Ra Mas?

DANI. I'm like on the waiting list.

DOTTIE. "Know and embody your circle." He said that.

(From above, there is the sound of the crowd stamping their FEET. Some PLASTER DUST drops down.)

BIGMAN. (*Looks up.*) What the hell the girls doin' up there?

DOLLY. (*Slapping herself in the head as SHE looks in the mirror.*) This don't look right!

DOTTIE. Money, money, money, money, money, money, money.

DANI. Shut up.

DOTTIE. (*Immediately completely focused on her.*) Lace up my shoe.

DANI. You got granola for brains, bitch.

BIGMAN. (*Seeing DOLLY rise meaningfully from her table.*) Lace up her shoe.

DANI. You lace up her shoe.

BIGMAN. Don't screw with me, Dani. Lace up her shoe!

(DANI laces up Dottie's shoe.)

DOTTIE. See some of us *are* desire, and some of us *serve* desire.

DANI. And some of us have our heads up our ass.

(BIGMAN immediately kicks her in the behind with the flat side of his shoe.)

DANI. Ow.

BIGMAN. You havin' a hard time understandin' me? You got a mouth ought to be washed out with soap.

DANI. I'll think it over.

(BIGMAN turns away, SHE immediately kicks him. HE turns.)

DANI. I thought it over.

TIGER. (*To Bigman.*) Go easy.

(At this moment LESSA re-enters, she is hot. NETTY follows. You can hear CROWD disorder in the background.)

LESSA. Hey, Bigman! They got some guy out there shootin' crap at me ... who knows ... a blow pipe. Hit me with a rock or ball bearing or some low-down shit ...

NETTY. Jesus, Bigman.

BIGMAN. (*To Tiger and Dani.*) You see what you got started out there?

LESSA. Coulda put my eye out ...

BIGMAN. And?

LESSA. An I went out after him.

BIGMAN. Outta the ring?

LESSA. I'm tellin' you I went out after him so nobody else has to tell you, an I'll go out after him again ...

LESSA. BIGMAN.

If I ever see him anywhere near ringside the rest of the night ...

I got one, only one rule, you don't go into the crowd under no circumstances no matter what.

NETTY. Got a bunch of animals out there, Bigman.

BIGMAN. Stay *in* the ring!

LESSA. Grabbed me out in the crowd started feelin' me up!

BIGMAN. ... Got no business leavin' the ring!!

(Suddenly there is a GUNSHOT. EVERYONE turns. It is DOLLY sitting at her dressing table holding a 9mm pistol.)

DOLLY. Y'all are makin' a lot of noise. I like it real quiet when I'm puttin' on my lipstick.

DOTTIE. You can smear lipstick.

DOLLY. Ordinarily we got a little room to ourselves. But if we got to be in the barnyard with the hogs, then we like to make it clear who's the head hog.

DOTTIE. See beauty is serene. I wonder could anybody go get me a little plain water in this cup?

NOLA. I'll get it.

DOTTIE. You are so sweet.

NOLA. Could I ask where's your tarantula?

DOTTIE. (*Touching her arm.*) I set it free.

TIGER. You want a hit, Lessa?

LESSA. (*Pointing at Dolly. To Bigman.*) You putting up with this crap?

(NOLA exits passing MOTHER who enters carrying a program. LESSA begins to change to "The Mercenary," dressed in jungle fatigues with a bandolier of ammunition.)

MOTHER. We got dissatisfied customers, goddammit!

NETTY. Oh, oh.

MOTHER. What we got here is some piss poor *no control*. You got nut-bustin' males in a room, you got to dominate 'em!

BIGMAN. I am in knowledge of this.

LESSA. Nobody, nooooobody shoots shit at me when I'm workin'.

MOTHER. (*To Bigman.*) One rule only, keep the dogs on a leash.

BIGMAN. What I'm gonna do …

MOTHER. … is toss 'em raw meat.

LESSA. (*Emphatic but to herself.*) Nobody!

MOTHER. Who's on next?

BIGMAN. Tiger goin' on Lessa bein' "The Mercenary."

MOTHER. Well, that's real smart!

BIGMAN. I believe so.

MOTHER. (*Slapping him sharply.*) That oughta set off a riot, get us all killed.

TIGER. Hey, we do this every night.

(NOLA reenters with Coke cup of water for Dottie.)

BIGMAN. They ain't gonna …

MOTHER. You think you're in goddamn Minneapolis? (*CROWD roars.*) You probably got Klan out there, probably got skinheads, neo-fuckin' Nazis, general all purpose defectives, got you a nice mix.

LESSA. You got you a nice mix.

MOTHER. What's your name, honey?

LESSA. What's your name?

MOTHER. My name is Sara Mae Louellen Crocker, originally from the Crocker auto repair Crockers before I saw Fantasy Entertainment was the growth industry of the 90's.

LESSA. Angelessa.

MOTHER. You wanta get hurt?

LESSA. I done my job in fifteen states.

MOTHER. Well, Lessa, you can either bleach yourself white or buy yourself some permanent rest in Cementville, Tennessee. These people pay good money to see people they don't like get beat up by people they do like *inside* the ropes. They don't like smart people, they don't like rich people, they don't like Arabs, they don't like Jews, and they don't like you. So they come down here to drink beer an yell shit at you an then everybody goes home happy. Fantasy Entertainment. Well you broke the rules an went *outside the ropes* ... you went an got real an now you're fucked. (*CROWD roars.*)

(DANI chuckles.)

MOTHER. *(Hands Lessa a ten.)* Go back to the hotel buy yourself some skin cream an a magazine and let me get this straightened out. (*Big CROWD roar.*)

BIGMAN. O.K., get us some wrestlers.

MOTHER. Shut up.

BIGMAN. Shut up?

MOTHER. This crowd won't sit through much more, they want my girls.

BIGMAN. Shut up?

DOLLY. This eye shadow, Mama?

MOTHER. Needs more.

DOLLY. (*Angry with herself.*) I keep on gettin' it wrong!

DOTTIE. I'm gettin' a headache, Mama.

BIGMAN. This is *my* friggin tour! Now …

MOTHER. (*To Bigman.*) Send 'em out naked.

BIGMAN. (*Appalled.*) Do what?

MOTHER. Send some of your talent out naked, get the rubes' minds on their cocks. We're not workin' while their blood's up. I got inves*tors*. I got invest*ments*.

BIGMAN. I can't send my girls out naked!

MOTHER. Why not?

BIGMAN. Why not? Why not? This is America, that's why not!

MOTHER. (*To the Knockout Sisters.*) Pack it up and move it out. We're goin' home.

BIGMAN. We got a verbal contract!

MOTHER. Dream on, sucker!

BIGMAN. Those rubes'll get nuts.

DOTTIE. (*Passing him.*) You got her upset now.

BIGMAN. Give me five minutes …

DOLLY. You think we need this? We did a fuckin' hairspray commercial.

DANI. You got any balls, Bigman?

BIGMAN. Give me one miserable minute here ...

DOTTIE. You couldn't peddle this act to a dog show.

TIGER. Watch it!

BIGMAN. (*Grabbing Dolly's purse off the makeup table.*) Okay, ladies, let's see what we got here ... (*HE dumps the contents on the ground.*)

DOLLY. Hey, dickwad ...

BIGMAN. (*Snatching something up.*) Oh, yes.

DOLLY. Hey!

BIGMAN. Seems to be ... (*Taking it out of her reach.*) Uh-uh. Seems to be white powder ...

DOLLY. You dumped my personal items ...

BIGMAN. In a little bitty glacine bag.

DOLLY. ... out my bag.

MOTHER. Bigman ...

BIGMAN. Might be say an illegal substance ...

MOTHER. You got both feet in your mouth ...

BIGMAN. ... be a real no-no seein' you're one day outta the joint.

(DOLLY slams trunk lid closed.)

MOTHER. Gettin' Dolly excited ...

BIGMAN. See just who is *head hog*!

DOTTIE. What you are holdin', sir, is a personal memento.

BIGMAN. What I'm holdin', bitch, is a trip back inside. (*To the wrestlers.*) You girls ever seen this shit before?

TIGER. (*Seeing Dolly pull out the pistol.*) Watch it!

DOLLY. (*Moving toward him with her pistol.*) *You* ever seen this shit before? (*DOLLY jams the gun against Bigman's nostrils.*)

DANI. O.K., O.K., we're messin' around while the rubes is trashin' the joint.

(LESSA laughs.)

BIGMAN. You think this is funny?

LESSA. Uh-huh.

DOLLY. Let's see you eat it.

BIGMAN. I ain't eatin' this.

MOTHER. Dolly, you are so unstable, honey.

DOLLY. Eat it.

DOTTIE. You want him to eat your precious memento?

NETTY. You think maybe we could get past the gun part?

DOLLY. Eat it!

TIGER. She's got fucked up eyes, Bigman.

NOLA. I could get us all some Coca Colas.

DOLLY. I been in a snuff film, pig snot. It was widely distributed.

DOTTIE. Money, money, money, money, money, money, money.

DOLLY. One, two ...

(CROWD roars.)

BIGMAN. (*Tosses the powder back, immediately chokes and spits it out.*) Choking ...

NETTY. Pound him.

(DANI and NOLA whack him on the back.)

DANI. Spit it out. Get rid of it.

(DOLLY has gone back to the makeup table lowering the pistol.)

NETTY. Whack him some more.
BIGMAN. Sand.
NETTY. Say what, honey?
MOTHER. You a little accident-prone, Bigman.
BIGMAN. That shit was sand. What the hell you carryin' sand around for in a little bag?
DOTTIE. May I share with him, Dolly?
DOLLY. You share with him.
DOTTIE. On July 16, 1985 …
BIGMAN. *(To Nola.)* Get me some water.
DOTTIE. I was at Daytona Beach with Dolly's husband Earl. Now the sky was a real pure teal blue …
BIGMAN. (*To Mother.*) We need wrestlin', for God's sake, what are we doin'?
DOTTIE. … just that single instant between day and dusk when time is suspended …

(A young WOMAN, perhaps sixteen, in an Andy Frane usher's uniform with a thin line of blood coursing across her face from a cut in her hairline, appears in the doorway. SHE smiles.)

MISS HARMON. Mr. Vague?

BIGMAN. Holy Jesus.

MISS HARMON. Paging Mr. Vague, please?

BIGMAN. What?

MISS HARMON. Mr. Vague?

BIGMAN. Vag.

MISS HARMON. Mr. Vag? Oh boy, oh boy, Mr. Vag.

NETTY. You're bleeding, honey.

MISS HARMON. (*Oblivious.*) Uh-huh.

DOTTIE. Oooooo, I hate that.

MISS HARMON. Mr. Vag, Mr. McClendon, the referee, he said, oh boy, here I wrote it down … we better get him some wrasslers pretty pronto, because that crowd, it's ugly, it's a real ugly crowd. It is. So, oh boy, that's the whole thing, the whole message. From Mr. McClendon. 'Cause they're about to shit a brick, Mr. Vag, they really are. So perhaps I could … I could bring him your perspective.

BIGMAN. Godammit, I'm just tryin' to make a living!

MISS HARMON. (*Writing.*) … Make a living.

BIGMAN. I got my brother in the hospital with his dick cut off!!

MISS HARMON. … Cut off.

BIGMAN. I got the Knockout Sisters from Screw Magazine feedin' me sand and the Cosa Nostra tellin' me to send my stable out naked an I got tanked up rubes trashin' uninsured property I'm gonna be responsible for …

MISS HARMON. Rubes?

BIGMAN. Now you tell me what the hell to do!?

(Irate CROWD sound.)

MISS HARMON. Well, I'm not sure, but they're throwing chairs.

NETTY. We ought to think this over, Bigman.

MOTHER. (*Steps forward. Wipes blood off the girl with her handkerchief.*) You tell him there is wrestlers comin'. Go on. Go on.

MISS HARMON. I will. Yes ma'am. Y'all, oh boy, y'all have a nice day, ya hear.

(Big CROWD sound.
SHE disappears. A moment.)

DOTTIE. (*Serenely.*) An I looked at Earl split by the horizon, with his history of impotence problems, standing there kind of give out, and I said, "Earl, I am Dolly and Dolly is me, we are the circle, we are the earth for you." An I lay down on the dusky beach and took him inside me and he cried out, "Dolly, Dolly, I'm home, Dolly." An then he had a heart attack and dropped dead.

DOLLY. Pretty much the way it always went.

DOTTIE. So I took some of that white sand from under his head and brought it home to Dolly as a memento which you have swallowed.

DOLLY. You hurt my heart.

TIGER. You got you some live ones, Bigman.

BIGMAN. I'm in charge here!

MOTHER. *(To Bigman.)* You want to know what to do?

BIGMAN. No!

(Big CROWD sound.
A moment. HE paces.)

BIGMAN. O.K., maybe.

NOLA. (*Entering.*) I got the water.

BIGMAN. (*Knocking the cup out of her hand.*) I never asked for any damn water.

NETTY. Biggie ...

MOTHER. You get the Indian ... (*Pointing at Dani.*) An the cowboy ... (*Pointing at Tiger.*) Out there in their underwear.

BIGMAN. I said that, I said underwear.

MOTHER. (*To Dottie.*) Hold it! We still got those garter belts?

DOTTIE. Oh, I'm just a little pack rat.

MOTHER. You announce you a specialty bout ... what did we call it that one time?

DOLLY. Bra wars.

DANI. Forget it.

DOLLY. You the Virgin Mary, huh?

DANI. I fuck but I don't tease.

MOTHER. Extra fifty dollars?

DANI. You can't find a whore for fifty dollars.

MOTHER. A c-note?

(SHE tosses it on the floor. LESSA reaches for it. DANI picks it up.)

DOLLY. Hard to find a *good* whore for a *hundred* dollars.

(SHE hands Dani two garter belts and stockings. DANI now changes from "Texas Gold" down to underwear, garter belt, stockings, and a sheer cover-up DOTTIE hands her.)

DANI. (*Mildly.*) You don't know what a whore is, babe. You livin' in blonde world. We just aren't playin' off the same sheet of music, toots. See, I'd rather be a hundred-dollar whore than a thousand-dollar blank. *(SHE walks away.)*

BIGMAN. (*Turning to Tiger.*) Tiger.

TIGER. You saw the bout. I been leanin' on this locker 'cause I can't get off it.

BIGMAN. O.K., Netty.

MOTHER. Those boys aren't lookin' for no ugly fat people in a G-string.

(HE turns to Lessa.)

NOLA. I can wrestle.

MOTHER. Yeah?

NOLA. I can wrestle good.

MOTHER. How old are you?

NOLA. Nineteen.

MOTHER. Where you worked?

NOLA. The Whale.

MOTHER. Where?

NOLA. It's an independent gas station with skateboard service.

MOTHER. Wrestled. Where have you wrestled?

NOLA. No place. Since I was twelve I saw all the bouts in three hundred miles. Thursday nights I practice with Jadine.

BIGMAN. Jadine who?

NOLA. My cousin. She weighs one ninety.

MOTHER. What kind of underwear you got on?

NOLA. Black with a red heart.

MOTHER. You're in the ring …

NOLA. Yeah.

MOTHER. She takes you down with a flying leg scissors …

NOLA. Yeah?

MOTHER. You do what?

NOLA. Counter with the grapevine, slip into a chicken wing and drop the heck out of her with a Carolina slam.

MOTHER. (*Holds out bills.*) Thirty bucks.

NOLA. I'm in? I'm in the bouts?

NETTY. You wanta do this, honey?

(CROWD roar.)

NOLA. I wanta wrassle. I wanta wrassle my ass off.

LESSA. Your mama oughta *whip* your ass.

NOLA. My mama already whips my ass. She whips my ass with a coat hanger.

BIGMAN. You do a good job there might be somethin' temporary on the tour.

NOLA. (*Beside herself.*) On the tour?

BIGMAN. See me up in my hotel room after the bouts? Number's ten-0-six.

NOLA. (*Looks at Netty.*) O.K., I'll be there. (*Leaps in the air, arm and fist extended.*) I am in! Yes! Get down!

BIGMAN. Right, that's settled.

NOLA. (*To Mother.*) What's my name?

MOTHER. Frenchy.

NOLA. All right!

(NOLA begins to undress. SHE gets ready to go out in her underwear plus garter belt, stockings and sheer cover-up handed to her by DOTTIE.)

TIGER. (*To Nola.*) Have a hit.

(NOLA takes one.)

LESSA. (*To Bigman.*) I got to have my money.

NOLA. Yes!

MOTHER. Let's get us some wrestlers in the ring.

(There is a flurry of activity as NOLA and DANI get ready.)

MOTHER. O.K., main event …

BIGMAN. Yes ma'am, now what we're gonna do is …

MOTHER. Shut up.

BIGMAN. I'm just saying …

MOTHER. Shut up. You tried to leverage me, now you're warm piss. You wanta wake up in your water bed with a fresh cut horse's head, you keep talkin'.

DOLLY. That was a good movie. (*Angry.*) I could *be* in that movie!

MOTHER. (*Pointing at Nola and Dani.*) I want the same two ...

LESSA. Wait a minute ...

MOTHER. ... in the main event.

DANI. (*Gives Lessa the finger.*) Hey, Lessa?

NETTY. (*Points at Nola.*) Now, Frenchy gonna be tired, and she's green.

(The USHER appears again in the doorway. A thin MAN in a black suit, white shirt, black string tie with a haunted face and a burr haircut has her by the hair.)

MISS HARMON. Mr. Vag, there is a gentleman to see you, Mr. Vag.

THE MAN. How y'all doin'?

BIGMAN. Get your hands off my staff.

(The MAN flicks open a switchblade in his free hand.)

MISS HARMON. Oh, no.

THE MAN. I'm Mr. One-Eye Deneauve down from Lecher County, Kentucky for the wrasslin'.

MOTHER. (*Moves up beside Bigman.*) Hello, One-Eye.

THE MAN. I drove a distance to see me some gut-pumpin', butt-bumpin', airborne wild pussy in a good family entertainment type show. See I hump two-hundred pound cartons all week so I'm seekin' an action attraction an I got squat zip right to this point.

MOTHER. I'm Mother Crocker, One-Eye, you probably seen me on the T.V.

THE MAN. Yes ma'am.

MOTHER. Seems like you got some sweet child by the hair there.

THE MAN. Could be. Now we don't get us some fine tits an see us some body fluids on the mat pretty quick, we gonna have to come down here cut out your pumpin' heart an eat that sumbitch like a nacho.

MOTHER. (*Walks up to within two inches of the man's face.*) One-Eye, we got some fine tits comin' up, an y'all aren't a hunnert percent satisfied you can have any woman in this room in a heart-shaped bed with mirrors on the ceiling all expenses paid an no questions asked, but you cut the girl here you gonna be one dead fuck. How's that sound?

THE MAN. You got a deal. (*HE releases Miss Harmon. HE winks and clicks his tongue, looking at Dottie.*) You a fine woman, Mama. I'll check on back. (*HE's gone.*)

MISS HARMON. (*Nervous but determined.*) I could have handled the situation. I got personnel training.

(The CROWD begins stamping and clapping.)

DANI. Why do I do this?

MOTHER. You want to stay down here?

MISS HARMON. Well, they need me in B Section non-reserved.

(There is a burst of SCREAMING from above.)

MISS HARMON. Oh, boy ... (*SHE exits, closing the door behind her. PEOPLE exhale.*)

DOTTIE. I'm not fuckin' him. I got standards.

LESSA. (*Steps forward.*) Lemme do the main. I got the know-how. I got the experience. I can handle your girls like they was marked fragile. I'm not goin' out in the crowd again. I will ... I will apologize to ... to the crowd. I'm a professional athlete, that's all I am and I need this work. I can make your girls look good. I can take punishment. If I have to do it I can take a straight punch. I uh ... I know how to take orders, do what I'm told. I'm askin' for the fight.

MOTHER. Angelessa?

LESSA. Yeah?

MOTHER. If you're in tennis, you're a professional athlete ...

LESSA. Yeah?

MOTHER. ... if you're in track and field, you're a professional athlete, even if you catch on with the Harlem Globetrotters, you're a professional athlete, but if you're in Fantasy wrestling in the main feature attraction they pay for, you are nothing in this world ...

DOLLY. But a nigger.

(LESSA steps toward her but BIGMAN gives her a two-handed push that sends her crashing into the lockers.)

NETTY. Lessa! Go easy now, go easy!

LESSA. (*Steadies herself against the lockers and leans there.*) I'm cool.

MOTHER. (*To Bigman.*) Take the girls out there.

NETTY. I don't know, Bigman.

BIGMAN. Dani, Frenchy, let's move it.

(CROWD roars.
HE exits. DOTTIE and DOLLY remove their cover-ups, revealing red, white and blue sequin peekaboo outfits with five-inch heels.)

DANI. (*Hesitates a moment, then:*) O.K. We pull hair, kick each other, stuff like that. Work the crowd. You pull off my top. I pull off yours. I mess you up with the Argentine. I full press, it's over. We grab the clothes, we're out of there. Six, eight minutes max.

NOLA. Just lead me.

DANI. You got it.

NOLA. (*To Tiger.*) Thanks.

TIGER. Don't mention it.

(NOLA and DANI exit.)

NETTY. I don't know ...

MOTHER. She's got tits, how bad can it be? (*Handing Bigman a xeroxed sheet.*) When they come off, hand 'em this. Breaks down how they wrestle my girls.

(BIGMAN takes it, starts to leave.)

MOTHER. Dottie doesn't work off her feet. I got those legs insured for thirty thousand.

DOTTIE. You said fifty.

MOTHER. Fifty. Nothin' in the face. They don't go through the ropes. Crowd gets messy, they split.

(BIGMAN starts out again. SHE stops him.)

MOTHER. Do right.

(BIGMAN exits.)

DOTTIE.	RING ANNOUNCER.
How do we look, Mama?	Gentlemen, we got a little change of program here …

MOTHER. Turn around.

DOTTIE. Do we look like queens, Mama? Are we sweet as pie?

MOTHER. I could eat you for breakfast.

DOLLY. Tryin' Passion Flower on my nails.

MOTHER. You look good.

DOTTIE. You look good too, Mama. You are part of the circle.

MOTHER. Stay away from the young one, she doesn't know shit.

DOLLY. No problem.

MOTHER. Stay off the ropes. I don't want you marked.

DOTTIE. Yes, Mama.

MOTHER. Smile to the crowd, they fans.

DOLLY. Yes, Mama.

MOTHER. (*Handing them miniature American flags.*) Wave the little flags.

DOTTIE. We will.

MOTHER. You are stars in the Fantasy Entertainment field.

DOLLY and DOTTIE. Yes, Mama.

MOTHER. We are just workin' out a little political setback ...

DOLLY. Yes, Mama.

MOTHER. Usin' drugs was a bad thing, a bad, bad thing.

DOTTIE. Yes, Mama.

MOTHER. But fuckin' the Mayor of Los Angeles was a good thing.

DOTTIE. Yes, mama.

MOTHER. That's part of a career. That's networking.

DOLLY. Yes, Mama.

MOTHER. All right, go on up there and get ready. Get inside yourselves.

DOTTIE. You didn't say we were goddesses, Mama.

MOTHER. You are motherfuckin' goddesses.

DOTTIE. (*Hugging her.*) You sweet ol' thing. (*Turns to the room.*) Bye, y'all. You keep evolving now, y'hear?

(SHE blows them a kiss and THEY are gone. We hear MUSIC and CROWD cheering.)

MOTHER. (*To those still in the room.*) Let me give you a little personal advice. Get yourself a husband and a shit job. You don't have it. You never will have it. You got no future on T.V. (*SHE leaves.*)

NETTY. How you feelin', Tiger?

TIGER. I'm feeling bad.

NETTY. You look bad. You want some morphine?

TIGER. You got?

NETTY. I got. (*A CROWD reaction. SHE reaches into her bag and pulls out a small commercial vial.*)

TIGER. Where you get it?

NETTY. Well, darlin', we have our little ways. (*CROWD roars.*)

TIGER. You always a surprise, ain't ya?

NETTY. Girl's got to live, honey.

TIGER. Hard as that may be. You got a syringe?

NETTY. (*Handing her one in a packet.*) Fresh as a daisy.

TIGER. (*Feeling her ribs.*) Makes my day.

NETTY. Cementville, Tennessee. I'm too fat for Fantasy Entertainment.

TIGER. An I'm too far out there. (*TIGER starts changing from Pocahontas back into street clothes.*)

NETTY. What about you, Lessa?

LESSA. Just fine.

NETTY. What you doin'?

LESSA. Gettin' dressed. (*LESSA puts on her Olympic warmup suit.*)

NETTY. Never saw you pull that out.

LESSA. Just seemed like what I wanted to wear.

TIGER. (*To dog.*) You sweet sweet thing.

NETTY. You want to catch a beer tonight?

LESSA. I'm catchin' a bus.

TIGER. Shit, Lessa, cool off.

LESSA. I'm cooled off. I'm way, way cooled off.

NETTY. Where you catchin' a bus to?

LESSA. Wherever seventeen dollars and change gets me.

NETTY. Probably Memphis. Shoot we're all goin' to Memphis. Get the bus with us in the mornin'.

LESSA. I don't think so.

(An old MAN, in his late sixties, early seventies, cane in hand appears in the doorway. He is African American.)

KID. Good evening.

NETTY. (*Caught off guard, SHE startles.*) Good Lord!

KID. Didn't mean to make you jump. (*Takes off his hat.*) Pay my respects.

LESSA. What do you need?

KID. Well, ladies, I don't have much and I don't need much.

TIGER. This here is a dressin' room. We got a show on, Granpa.

KID. (*Points to a poster.*) Willie "The Kid" Cayman, that's my picture.

(THEY look. HE laughs.)

NETTY. This is you, honey?

KID. Light on my feet. Lookin' real sweet. TNT in both hands.

NETTY. Honey, you got million dollar charm.

KID. Much obliged.

NETTY. Don't mention it. (*ROARING and WHISTLING from the crowd.*)

KID. Could I bother you ladies to step in? On my way from Key West, Florida to Catafalque Bay, Alaska in a '79 Cadmium Red Pontiac Firebird. Stoppin' here, stoppin' there.

NETTY. Come on in, darlin'.

KID. Just call me Kid. (*Turns to Tiger.*) Kid Cayman.

TIGER. Tiger.

KID. Tiger who?

TIGER. Just one name.

KID. (*Smiling.*) Uh-huh, I can understand that. (*Sees cat case.*) I got me a small yellow dog. (*Turns to Lessa.*) Seems to me I know you, sister.

RING ANNOUNCER. ... winner of our lingerie interlude, lusty, busty Dani Malowsky!

(*CROWD reaction.*)

LESSA. I don't think so.

KID. Sure I do. I got a memory they come miles for.

LESSA. Angelessa.

KID. Oh, it'll come to me. I'm workin' on it. (*The crowd breaks into APPLAUSE.*) You're all in the wrestlin' bouts, huh?

NETTY. That's right, honey.

KID. Now I had one hundred seventy fights, featherweight to middleweight, but I still got my brains 'cause they couldn't hit me. I was kinda here, kinda gone at the same time. What you'd call a will-of-the-wisp. (*To Lessa.*) Your daddy wasn't the cut man for Sugar Ray Robinson, was he? (*SHE shakes her head.*) Fought here two times. Once with Jose Higuera, an old veteran with a good left hand. Carried him eight rounds so he could set up another payday. Once with Sandy Sadler. Oh, he was the dirtiest fighter alive, thumbed me so bad. Took forty-six stitches 'round my left eye. Knocked me down seven times. It's in the book. Fought Sandy three times. (*To Lessa.*) You ever won a beauty contest?

LESSA. Kid, I never won a beauty contest.

KID. Well, the fix musta been in. You ever married to a high hurdler?

(Crowd ROARS, APPLAUDS and WHISTLES.)

LESSA. (*Smiling.*) You ought to move on pretty soon, Kid.

KID. Oh, I plan to. Yes, you got to keep movin'. (*Looks around room.*) Oh my, ladies ... memory lane.

(At this moment DANI and NOLA enter like whirlwinds. THEY have covered themselves with the kimonos. THEY change into ninja costumes for the main event. THEY have masks.)

NOLA. Whoa! Hot patootie, was that somethin'?

DANI. Into it, honey! I'll say that for them.

NOLA. … Throwin' money …

DANI. Bills …

NOLA. Change, bills, I didn't have a …

DANI. Five dollar bills …

NOLA. … Have a place to tuck it …

DANI. (*Passing Kid.*) Who's he?

KID. Bon jour, how you doin'?

TIGER. Used to fight here.

DANI. Pop, you got my sympathies. (*Handing money to Netty.*) Eighty bucks off the floor. Split it up.

(TIGER starts humming "Me and My Shadow," occasionally singing a few words of the lyric.)

NOLA. Am I gettin' this on straight?

NETTY. Come over here, honey.

DANI. How you doin', Tiger?

TIGER. Feelin' no pain.

DANI. (*Holding up xeroxed sheets Mother gave Bigman.*) You see this shit? The Dolly & Dottie Show.

NETTY. How it goes?

DANI. Yeah, how it goes. They parade around, we fall down. They writhe around on the floor, we're amazed. Va-Va-Voom, we collapse unconscious.

LESSA. Damn.

DANI. Fuckin' stupid. Tiger, dammit! (*TIGER stops singing.*) Well, you got to play it like it lays.

LESSA. Get goin'.

DANI. I'm gone.

NOLA. (*Tying the laces.*) One minute.

DANI. (*Exiting.*) Catch you up there.

NOLA. (*Finishing.*) I am sweatin' buckets.

RING ANNOUNCER. And now our featured bout of the evening ... the fine, fabulous femmes fatales of American wrestling ... direct from national television ...

LESSA. Lemme look you over.

NOLA. (*Moves over to her.*) I hope I can do this.

LESSA. Turn around.

(NOLA does. LESSA pushes her into the broom closet and slams the door, turns the twist lock. TIGER chuckles.)

NOLA. Hey!

NETTY. Now, Lessa ...

NOLA. (*From inside.*) Come on, Lessa. I got to get up there. Stop playin' around.

LESSA. The bitch as called me a nigger is mine.

NOLA. Let me outta here! I got to be wrasslin', I can't be in here.

NETTY. Lessa, what the hell ...

LESSA. Payback.

NETTY. Don't be crazy now.

LESSA. I'm gone.

(SHE moves rapidly to the outside door. Just as she gets there, two hands fasten on her throat and drive her back into the room. It is EDDIE. HE wears a hospital robe over hospital pajamas. There is some blood staining

through his bandages and onto the robe. EDDIE is big. His face is gray. His voice a gurgle in his throat. He's a little like the Frankenstein monster only he moves faster.)

EDDIE. You bit my dick off. (*HE drives her up against the wall.*) You … bit … my … dick off.

NETTY. Eddie … come on, Eddie.

(LESSA fights, but HE maintains the grip.)

EDDIE. Bit … bit my … dick.

TIGER. (*Trying to move.*) Get him off her.

(EDDIE makes only a gurgling roar now. HE bends Lessa backward over the bench.)

NETTY. Come on, Eddie. Come on, Eddie.

(A very loud voice cuts across the ruckus. It is KID.)

KID. Stosha!! Stosha "The Wild Man" Oronovsky!

(EDDIE throws Lessa down and turns. The KID opens his arms with a radiant smile.)

KID. You the cream in my coffee, man.

(KID slaps his own hand and holds it out. EDDIE, trancelike, slaps it and THEY are into a six or eight

beat streetshake at the end of which the KID drives his knee upward into Eddie's groin. EDDIE lets out pain that lasts an eternity. When he stops the KID says:)

KID. You slicker than a snake on ice, baby.

(EDDIE crashes to the floor insensate. Unfortunately HE falls on Tiger's cat box. Tiger doesn't see it. NETTY does.)

NETTY. Oh God!
TIGER. You O.K., Lessa?
LESSA. Yeah. I'm fine. Stay off me.

(The KID turns to LESSA who has stumbled to her feet.)

KID. Did you ever put the shot in Seoul, Korea?
LESSA. (*Nods.*) Down in Seoul, Korea.
KID. Ooooooo, you were fine! Now you go on up there and have a good time. I like to see people enjoy themselves.

(LESSA nods and moves out of the room.)

TIGER. How'd you know his ring name?
KID. Read the poster on the way in. I got me a memory I could point out the same fly five days apart.
TIGER. You think he's hurt bad?
KID. (*A big smile.*) He might be if she bit his dick off.
TIGER. (*Sings lightly.*) "Walkin' down the avenue ..."
NETTY. Tiger honey, I got bad, bad news.

TIGER. What?

NETTY. Well, he fell on your dog.

TIGER. Where?

NETTY. Kind of flush, direct *on* her. (*SHE kneels by Eddie and lifts his upstage side a little.*) Oh my. Tiger darlin', I'm afraid she passed.

TIGER. Yeah? (*NETTY nods.*) O.K.

NETTY. Honey, I'm sorry.

TIGER. (*Tears rolling down her cheek.*) O.K.

NOLA. *(Pounding on the door.*) Let me outta here!!

NETTY. Oh my God, I forgot. (*Heads for the closet.)*

KID. Let her cool down.

TIGER. (*Trying to get up.*) Whoa, got the nods.

KID. No last name, huh?

TIGER. No name.

KID. You know what I see when I look in your eyes, Tiger?

TIGER. Yeah, what?

KID. Morphine. Morphine, am I right?

TIGER. Yeah.

KID. Oh, that's a sweet low, isn't it? I had me several months of that down in Calcutta. Oh I'd cry and I'd cry and I'd sleep like a baby.

(There is an ugly ROAR from the crowd upstairs.)

TIGER. We're all fucked.

NETTY. We are.

KID. Not me, I got Florida real estate.

NETTY. I hope Bigman don't hurt her.

TIGER. Yeah.

NETTY. (*To Tiger who is throwing stuff in a bag.*) What are you doin'?

TIGER. Movin' out. (*Starts tossing stuff in the flight bag.*)

NETTY. You got no place to go.

TIGER. I can go where that crowd ain't. (*Another ROAR.*) Fuck this place.

NETTY. (*Looking down at Eddie.*) One thing, Lessa, she'll be gone.

TIGER. Eddie don't look like he's wrestlin' in Memphis.

NOLA. Tiger? Somebody? (*There is a tremendous ROAR from upstairs.*)

KID. (*Looking at the ceiling.*) Uh-huh, they like it.

TIGER. (*Looking around the room.*) Ain't much works out.

KID. I had an uncle lost his greeting card business, on the next day, the next day he won an *all expenses paid vacation* for two in Hawaii.

NETTY. That ain't us, oldtimer.

KID. Outside his hotel he put fifty cents in a machine to get a papaya juice an the can got stuck. He shook that machine and it tipped over on him, broke both his legs.

TIGER. Sure, it works that way.

KID. In that hospital he met a beautiful nurse who a year after became his wife …

NETTY. You're kiddin'?

KID. That's right, two years after that she poisoned him for his insurance. Oh, you never know what's coming off next.

(There is SHRIEKING in the hall and moments later DOTTIE appears holding one hand over her face. Her head and face seem covered with blood.)

DOTTIE. My face! Oh God, my face. My eye. Where's my eye?

NETTY. Jee-sus.

DOTTIE. (*Trying to see the damage in the makeup table mirror.*) I'm ruint. Ruint in the race wars. My God, I can't see out of my eye.

NETTY. Let me look.

DOTTIE. (*Raging.*) I got to be in the movies!

NETTY. Sit still! Where's your sister?

DOTTIE. Went under. Some thyroid giant drug her into the crowd by one leg. I seen somebody rip off her G-string an eat it. They've gone crazy.

NETTY. Looks like it's mainly the nose.

DOTTIE. (*Shrieking.*) Oh Jesus, I'm disfigured!

(LESSA enters, she has MOTHER, her dress ripped and completely disheveled, in a headlock.)

MOTHER. Three hundred dollars.

(LESSA bangs Mother's head into a locker.)

MOTHER. Six hundred dollars.

TIGER. Hi there, Lessa.

(LESSA bangs Mother into the lockers again.)

LESSA. (*To Tiger.*) How you doin'?
MOTHER. You bitch, you tore my artificial breast off. (*MOTHER pulls free.*)
LESSA. So long, Mama.

(SHE hits her cleanly with a punch. MOTHER goes down.)

NETTY. Godammit, stop roughhousin'!
TIGER. Bye, Netty.
NETTY. Hold on.
TIGER. Adios, Bigman.

(BIGMAN enters, his shirt is torn, his suit jacket a collage of spilled coke, crackerjacks and beer. He's obviously been on the floor in the arena.)

BIGMAN. (*Acknowledges her without thinking.*) Yeah.
DOTTIE. Is that a broken nose?
TIGER. Lef' three cans of gourmet dog food.
DOTTIE. My God, that's a broken nose.

(TIGER exits. BIGMAN focuses on Lessa.)

BIGMAN. You have screwed with my hustle. You miserable slimeball, five-way cunt.

(LESSA charges him knocking him down. For the first moment of the fight SHE seems to dominate him. SHE gets him in a hammerlock. HE breaks it. Slowly the fight begins to change. Soon BIGMAN dominates. Then HE begins to administer a real beating. HE brutalizes Lessa. It must look like HE might actually kill her. During the fight other dialogue takes place.)

NETTY. Lessa! Lessa, for Christ's sake, blow it off! Lessa!

DOTTY. (*Over to the fallen Mother.*) Mama, she broke my nose, Mama.

NETTY. Bigman!

BIGMAN. (*To Netty.*) Off me.

DOTTIE. There'll be media, Mama. We got to go. We can't be on the T.V. all ruint. Come on, Mama. (*SHE pulls at her.*) My God, it's the apocalypse. (*Pulling her to the door.*) They ate Dolly, Mama. They like cannibals, Mama.

BIGMAN. (*Beating Lessa.*) Yes. Oh yes. Oh yes.

DOTTIE. Come on, Mama. I got you. I got you, Mama. (*Pulls her out the doorway and exits.*)

(BIGMAN slams Lessa against the lockers. SHE falls down. Without warning, and from where he sits, the KID shoots him with Dolly's gun. BIGMAN sits

suddenly down, awkwardly, as if surprised. The room freezes. Sound from the arena where a full-scale RIOT is in progress rocks around them.)

BIGMAN. Who shot me? (*HE focuses on the Kid.*) You shot me. (*HE sees Eddie.*) What's Eddie doin' here? Christ, he shot Eddie. You're a serial killer.

(LESSA lurches to her feet; feels if she's in working order; crosses to bucket of water. Throws some on face.)

NETTY. (*Looking at the carnage.*) You O.K., Lessa?

DANI. (*Enters.*) The rubes they ... unbelievable ... on the floor, in the ring, like a bee swarm ... broke pipes, water gushin' in ... I'm tellin' ya ... the rubes gone apeshit ... *(Sees Bigman, Eddie.)* What the hell?

BIGMAN. I'm shot. I'm shot down.

NETTY. Let me see.

BIGMAN. Get off me!

(LESSA still in a rage trashes the sisters' makeup tables. Sweeps tubes and bottles onto the floor. Rips tables away from the wall and upends them.)

LESSA. Yes!!!

DANI. Goddammit, Lessa.

(LESSA opens the Knockout Sisters' trunk, goes through the clothes, flings them around room.)

DANI. (*To Bigman.*) Who shot you?

BIGMAN. (*Vastly irritated.*) Who gives a shit? I'm shot.

DANI. (*Indicating the Kid.*) Are you still here?

KID. Just passin' through.

DANI. Is that Eddie? Eddie, is that you?

NETTY. Jesus.

LESSA. Sequins, man. I hate sequins.

DANI. (*SHE checks Eddie.*) Jesus. This ain't my style. We got to blow, Netty, we got to blow now. (*GLASS breaks somewhere outside the door.*) You hear that? The rubes are comin'. (*Turns to Kid.*) Don't shoot. Don't shoot me.

KID. (*Chuckling.*) O.K.

LESSA. (*Surveying the damage she has wrought.*) Lookin' good.

(NOLA pounds on the door. DANI startles.)

NETTY. Oh, God.

DANI. Who is it? What is that?

NETTY. I completely ... (*SHE unlocks door.*)

DANI. We got Dwayne again?

NOLA. (*Emerging.*) I been ... no air ... banging. I been yelling ... (*SHE sees.*) Jeeminy, holy cow, boy-Friday.

(LESSA packs her stuff.)

DANI. Now. Out now.

(More CRASHES outside. DANI throws stuff in her bag. SHE scoops up the money from her fight with Nola. NETTY kneels by Bigman.)

DANI. There's gonna be cops and bad shit.

NOLA. We're gonna die, we're all gonna die.

NETTY. You want me to stay, Bigman? (*SHE touches him, HE yells.*) Sorry.

BIGMAN. That hurt, O.K.?

DANI. (*To Netty.*) Let's roll. Come on, Netty.

NETTY. (*Back to Bigman.*) Poor darlin'.

BIGMAN. Will you get your fingers out of the bullet hole?

NETTY. Bigman.

BIGMAN. You could kill a fuckin' tree.

DANI. (*Pulling Netty away.*) Cops, Netty, freaked out rubes ... (*Gestures at the fallen bodies.*) They gonna pin this shit on us.

KID. Say ...

DANI. (*Whirling.*) Don't even look at me.

KID. Kid Cayman ... How you doin'?

DANI. Screw off.

(Angry CROWD burst.)

DANI. (*A sudden thought.*) You got a car, Pop?

KID. A car, huh?

DANI. A drivable car.

KID. Got me a '79 Cadmium Red Pontiac Firebird parked right out front in a handicapped zone.

LESSA. You lookin' for company?

KID. Always lookin' for company. Got a workin' radio, a part-time clock, and she seats six comfortable. (*Tosses her the keys.*) Pull it in the back; I'll be along.

LESSA. (*Looking at him.*) O.K.

KID. Don't mention it. Ooooooo, you was poetry in motion!

(PEOPLE are standing around.)

DANI. Are you all like *deranged?* Let's split.

NETTY. Where?

DANI. When the hell did we ever know where?

(LESSA moves out without speaking.)

DANI. Move it. Hump it. Move it.

NETTY. (*Taking the terrified Nola's hand.*) Come on, honey. Mama take care of you.

DANI. (*Pulls and pushes Nola and Netty out.)* Move it. Move it. Beat it. Go! Go! Beat it. Beat it!

(NOLA and NETTY exit.)

LESSA. Eddie. Hey Eddie.

(HE suddenly shoots out a hand and grabs her ankle.)

LESSA. Let go.

(HE doesn't. HE tries to pull her over. SHE stamps on his wrist. HE lets go with a grunt. SHE goes down on one knee just outside his grasp.)

LESSA. I hope you don't die, but I hope you come goddamn close. Amen. (*SHE rises.*)

DANI. (*Speaks to Kid.)* Hell, that oughta make him feel better.

(LESSA exits.)

DANI. So long, Bigman.

BIGMAN. Get me some help.

DANI. (*Ambivalently.*) Sure. (*To Kid.*) Move it out, Pops. (*SHE exits.*)

(KID rises and closes the hall door. HE twist-locks it. We hear the sound of the approaching CROWD.)

BIGMAN. You snuffed me.

KID. You won't die. I didn't hit you in the right spot. (*Looks at Eddie.*) I hit him in the right spot.

EDDIE. ... My dick.

KID. Uh-huh. (*To Bigman.*) You Jack Vag's boy, used to be a coffee kid down to Joe Louis Gym.

(BIGMAN looks at him amazed.)

KID. Now you doin' this trash.

BIGMAN. What the hell are *you* doin'?

KID. Keepin' you company.

(CRASH from outside.)

BIGMAN. Don't ditch me.

KID. You want a smoke?

BIGMAN. Yeah.

KID. Hurtin' people, now that's a serious gig, see. I don't play with it. I don't fool nobody. (*Big smile.*) When I hurt 'em, I hurts 'em. (*Puts the cigarette in Bigman's mouth.*) I ever tell you I fought Sandy Sadler three times? Second fight a woman come to the dressing room, bare shoulders, ball gown, took off a diamond bracelet, give it to me, said, "You, sir, gave a fine account of yourself." (*HE tips over a bank of lockers, stage right. Points at a door behind the locker which has been revealed.*) Come right through there in that China silk dress. Took me to her home on a bluff overlooked a wide turn in the Mississippi and there we danced the Samba to a sixteen-piece all-girl orchestra from Venezuela. Sandy Sadler, he was there. Two-Ton Tony Galento, he was in town. Ooooo, he was light on his feet. The referee, he danced with the Governor's wife and a Secret Service man. Ol' Jake Lamotta, he slow danced with a nine-year-old girl standin' on his shoes. Oh, that was a sight. The waiters in their white coats, they joined in. All of us laughin', hummin' along, all doing the rumba, while the moon went down. (*HE heads out.*) There was a girl playin' clarinet in that band later left a camelia on my pillow. (*His voice recedes down the hall.*) 'Course those were different times. Different times. Different times.

(A moment. Someone begins POUNDING on the hall door. We hear, "Y'all in there ... you're road kill, you hear me." BIGMAN startles awake.)

BIGMAN. Eddie?
EDDIE. Yeah?
BIGMAN. You there?
EDDIE. Yeah?
BIGMAN. How much you got left?

(No answer. The LIGHTS start to fade. A fire AXE breaks through the panel of the door. Once, twice, a third time. The LIGHTS are out.)

THE END

COSTUME PLOT

Offstage (In dressing room)

TIGER

tank top, jeans/belt, jean jacket (w/logo), shoes (Dr. Scholl sandals), underwear, dance bra, flesh tights, Pocahontas dance pants/loin cloth, Pocahontas halter, Pocahontas kneepads, Pocahontas boots

DANI

G-string undies, white shirt, blue jeans w/belt, socks, boots, beret, earrings, watch, neck chain/padlock w/key, bra (Texas Gold), Texas Gold leotard

LESSA

bra, undies, pullover sweatshirt, sweatpants, socks, high-top sneakers

NETTY

bra/undies, T-shirt, jeans, hooded sweatshirt w/zipper, socks, shoes, eyeglasses, Pajama Mama makeup

NOLA

bra & black G-string panties, T-shirt, cut-off jeans, socks, sneakers,

DOTTIE

stretch dress, pantyhose, undies, high-heeled pumps, blonde wig, stripped leggings, sheer bodysuit/pasties, kimono, distressed striped leggings, distressed bodysuit/pasties, face blood & towel

DOLLY

stretch dress, pantyhose, undies, high-heeled pumps, blonde wig, striped leggings, sheer bodysuit/pasties, kimono, high-heeled lace-up boots

BIGMAN
Suit #1 (pants, jacket, tie,), shoes, socks, hat, hankie, wristwatch, Suite #2 - distressed, 1 pair of kneepads, 1 pair elbow pads
MOTHER
Suite #1 (skirt, jacket, blouse), shoes, stockings, jewelry, purse w/props, distressed skirt, blouse
MS. HARMON
usher suit, face blood
ONE-EYE
suit, aviator glasses
EDDIE
hospital gown, robe, shoes, IV tube & tape, hospital bracelet
DWAYNE
shirt, jeans, jacket, shoes, socks
KID
pants, shirt, jacket w/pocket, hat

Offstage for intermission preset

DOTTIE
high-heeled lace-up boots

Offstage in individual bags

TIGER
Bloody Mary padded bra, Bloody Mary lace-up boots, makeup bag w/ Pocahontas makeup
DANI
Tarzana wristlets, Tarzana headband, makeup bag w/makeup
LESSA
Bag #1: Mercenary tights, Mercenary wristlets, makeup bag w/makeup

Bag #2: Olympic warmup suit (pants & jacket), Mercenary kneepads

NETTY

PJ Mama wristlets, PJ Mama boots, PJ Mama socks, PJ Mama wig

In trunks

Trunk #1

LESSA

Black Lightning tights, Black Lightning leotard w/hood, gloves, lace-up boots, thigh walkie-talkie holder, black sunglasses

TIGER

Pocahontas wig/w/headband, Pocahontas blanket robe (to be set in lockers at intermission)

LESSA

Mercenary jungle pants/belt, Mercenary tank top, headband, shell sash (to be set in lockers at intermission)

Trunk #2

TIGER

Bloody Mary unitard, headband, kneepads

DANI

flesh tights, Tarzana unitard, belt, vest, wrist gauntlets, kneepads, cowboy boots, neckerchief, cowboy hat, Ninja top, Ninja pants, Ninja hood, Ninja shoes

NETTY

pink striped PJ bottoms & top

NOLA

Ninja top, Ninja pants, Ninja hood, Ninja shoes

Knockout trunk

DANI

garter belt/stockings, lace coverup, pumps
NOLA
garter belt/stockings, lace coverup, pumps
DOTTIE
sequin motorcycle jacket
DOLLY
sequin motorcycle jacket
Add'l sequined items

PROPERTY PLOT

locker banks (4)	bar lock (across bottom five lockers)
assorted trash in dressing room	shower room trash
closet trash	twist-locks (2)
ceiling light fixture	light switch (wall SR of hall door)
2 tires	5 gallon plastic bucket (sittable)
broken bench	posters
old soda can	army knapsack bag (Tiger)
cat case	chihuahua
break-away cat case	water bottle
comic books (2)	pushbroom
pack of cigarettes	matches
French fries in fast food container	1/2 eaten burrito
Dani's bag	Rag (to clean lockers)
plastic bottle of aspirin	dollar bills
Lessa's bags (2)	Walkman w/earphones
Netty's bag	pack of Black Jack gum
benches (2)	costume trunks (2)
first aid kit	Lg bottle of pills
sm. square mirrors (2)	1/2 roll of silver duct tape
6 pack of Corona beer	bucket w/water
makeup table	2 stools
1/2 pint of Wild Turkey	newspaper section
makeup bags	tape for mirrors
4 cans of gourmet dog food	autograph book, pen

Cigarillo
2 sm. makeup mirrors for KO sisters
Smirnoff bottle
war paint makeup
plaster dust/chips
pistol double
Coke cup
bandolier of ammo
eye shadow (Dolly)
sm. bag w/white powder
blood
water cup
$30 (Mother)
xeroxed sheets
vial of morphine
"The Kid" poster
IV tube/surgical tape
blood bag for gunshot wound
French cigarette pack
fire axe
can of Pepsi
bottle w/herb pills
money clip (Bigman)
2 pair of small scissors
2 sm. towels (Netty)
cold cream jar
sm. vase of flowers
stick incense & matches
icepack

trunk for KO sisters
locker dressing (Dottie)
brown paper bag
towel
9mm gun/blanks
lipstick
fight program
$10 bill
Dolly's purse w/items
hairbrush
pad & pen
$100 bill
switchblade
mini USA flags (2)
syringe in plastic packet
$80
face blood
car keys
lighter
breakable door panel
dead rose
box of Kleenex
compacts w/mirrors (2)
dental floss
picture in frame (Dottie's locker)
nail polish remover
sm. Buddha statue
old toothbrush (for eyebrows)
hairspray, mousse